SCOTLAND'S CHANGING LANDSCAPES

Kenneth Maclean

Principal Teacher of Geography, Perth Academy

and Norman Thomson

Formerly Head of Social Studies,
Moray House Institute, Edinburgh

Hodder & Stoughton

A MEMBER OF THE HODDER HEADLINE GROUP

Acknowledgements

The authors and publishers would like to thank the following for permission to reproduce materials in this book. Every effort has been made to trace and acknowledge all copyright holders, but if any have been overlooked the publishers will be pleased to make the necessary arrangements.

James Buchan, *The Expendable Mary Slessor*; B Kaye; Pringle of Scotland, for reproduction of their logo in Section 28; Scottish Cultural Press, *Teach Yourself Doric*, '*Look Faa's Here*', D Kynoch; Scottish Natural Heritage, for reproduction of their logo in Section 17; the verse from *Bennygoak* by Flora Garry appears in *Collected Poems*, Gordon Wright Publishing 1995

The authors would like to thank the following individuals and organisations for their help and advice in the preparation of this book.

James Armstrong, Luffness Farm; Mary Cameron, Headteacher, Kilchoan Primary; Donald Gillies, former Headteacher, Goodlyburn Primary, Perth; Barbara Hogarth, former Ranger, Ben Lawers; Gordon Jarvie; John Mackay; Hazel Maclean, Letham Primary, Perth; Joan Mann, former Headteacher, Balquhidder Primary; Jean Pringle, Perth Academy; Sarah Stewart, Dunaverig Farm.

Economic Development Departments, City of Edinburgh and Grampian Region; Farming and Wildlife Advisory Group; Forest Enterprise, Forest of Ae; Highlands and Islands Enterprise; Livingston Development Corporation; the National Trust for Scotland; Pringle of Scotland; Scottish Nuclear; Summerlee Heritage Centre.

With special thanks to Joanne Osborn for her patience and help.

The publishers would also like to thank the following for giving permission to reproduce copyright photographs in this book.

Dr Ian Armit, Figure 18.1; Caledonian Newspapers, Figures 1.7, 27.5, 28.3; J Allen Cash Ltd, Figures 22.1, 24.5, 24.7, 25.8; Colorific!, Figures 25.2, 30.5; Sylvia Cordaiy, Figure 10.5; Peter Davenport, Figure 28.2; Ecoscene, Figure 20.8; The Edinburgh Photographic Library, Figures 5.6, 7.2, 15.6; Louis Flood, Figure 10.6; FLPA, Figure 3.3, top, bottom middle and right; Forest Life, Figure 15.5; GSF Picture Library, Figure 3.3, bottom left; Robert Harding, Figure 7.5; Highlands and Islands Development Board, Figure 2.3; The National Trust for Scotland, Figures 17.10, 23.6; Panoramic of Torness, Figure 16.7; John Parker, Figure 30.8; The Scottish Highland Photo Library, Figures 2.4, 4.4 (Eric Thorburn), 5.4, 6.2, 7.1, 7.4, 21.7 (Eòlas), 21.8, 30.9; Scottish Hydro, Figure 16.7; Spanphoto, Figure 27.6; Still Moving Pictures, Paul Tomkins/STB, Figure 31.5; The Telegraph Colour Library, Figure 4.6; Topham Picturepoint, Figures 1.8, 3.1, 5.3, 10.7; David Williams Picture Library, Figures 6.5, 16.5, 22.1.

All other photos belong to the authors.

Cover artwork by Clive Goodyer.
Inside artwork by Joe McEwan, London and Bitmap Graphics, Berkhamsted.

Cataloguing in Publication Data is available from the British Library

ISBN 0 340 65500 3

First published 1995
Impression number 10 9 8 7 6 5 4 3 2 1
Year   1999 1998 1997 1996 1995

Copyright © 1995 Norman Thomson and Kenneth Maclean

Typeset by Litho Link Ltd, Welshpool, Powys, Wales.
Printed in Great Britain for Hodder & Stoughton Educational, a division of Hodder Headline Plc, 338 Euston Road, London NW1 3BH by Bath Press Colourbooks, Glasgow.

Contents

N.B. Glossary terms are in **bold** the first time they occur in the text.

Scotland and the Wider World

NAME: *Fiona Maclean*
STREET: *15 Coo Vennel*
TOWN/VILLAGE: *Auchtertarra*
COUNTRY: *Scotland*
CONTINENT: *Europe*
PLANET: *Earth*

Figure 1.1 A world address

This book is about Scotland, its people and their landscapes. By filling out as full an address as possible, we see that:

- Scotland is part of the British Isles, which are divided into five countries (see Figures 1.2 and 1.3);
- the British Isles lie north west of, and are part of, the continent of Europe;
- Europe is a triangular-shaped peninsula which points westwards from Asia. So Scotland is a very small part of a huge 'Eurasia'.

Figure 1.2 The United Kingdom and the Irish Republic

Figure 1.3 The British Isles

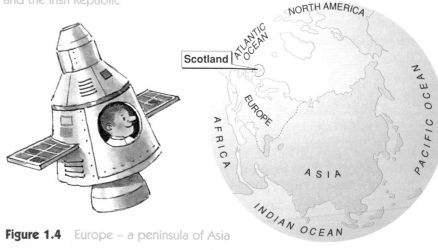

Figure 1.4 Europe – a peninsula of Asia

Scotland's Position

Scotland's position has been important throughout its history. In Roman times it was an isolated area on the north west frontier (Figure 1.5, map A). By Viking times, however, Orkney and Shetland were centrally placed for ships sailing to Ireland or Iceland (Figure 1.5, map B). In later years, partly as a result of wars with England, the burghs of the east coast traded with Europe (Figure 1.5, map C). By the eighteenth and nineteenth centuries, when Britain's main trade was across the Atlantic, Scotland was well placed to export to and import from North America. This position was very important in the growth of the ports of the Clyde estuary, especially Glasgow. Tobacco, sugar and cotton were among the imports from the USA and the West Indies. Street names such as Virginia Street remind us of this.

Figure 1.5 Map A:
The Roman Empire 100 AD

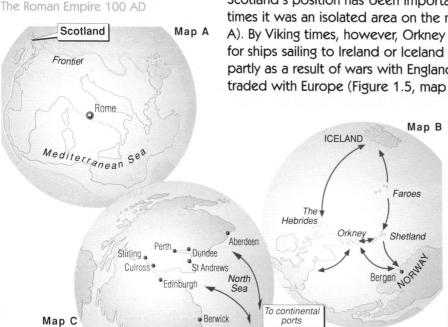

Map B: The Viking period 900AD   **Map C:** Medieval trade with the continent

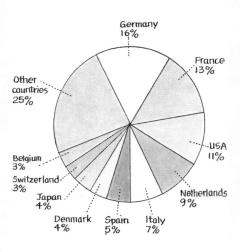

Figure 1.6   Where Scotland's exports go

Figure 1.7   Mossend freight terminal links Glasgow with the Channel Tunnel

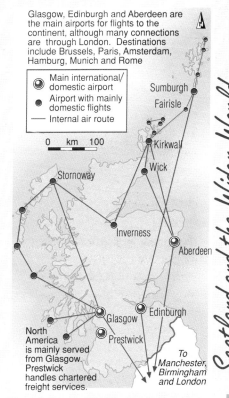

Glasgow, Edinburgh and Aberdeen are the main airports for flights to the continent, although many connections are through London. Destinations include Brussels, Paris, Amsterdam, Hamburg, Munich and Rome

North America is mainly served from Glasgow. Prestwick handles chartered freight services.

To Manchester, Birmingham and London

Figure 1.9   Scotland: air transport

Scotland and Europe Today

Scotland has many links with Europe, especially the countries of the EU, or European Union (see Figure 1.10).

- The pie chart in Figure 1.6 shows that most of Scotland's exports (whisky, electronics, textiles, etc) go to Europe. Germany and France are Scotland's two main customers.

- Scotland is now a lot closer to Europe than it used to be! In the seventeenth century, it took about five days to sail to the Netherlands. Today, Schipol airport near Amsterdam is only an hour's flight from Edinburgh. Thanks to domestic flights to the larger Scottish airports, the remoter parts of Scotland are also closer to Europe in terms of travelling times.

Figure 1.8   Glasgow Airport beside the M8 on the western edge of the city is Scotland's busiest airport

- With the opening of the Channel Tunnel in 1994, Britain is no longer an island. Direct rail links with the continent should be quicker now, although many lorries still use English ports such as Hull.

- Since the UK joined the EU, Scotland's landscapes have been affected by regulations from Brussels, for example:
  – lowland farmers can no longer produce so much in the way of crops and milk (see p 27);
  – fishermen are not allowed to catch so many fish (see p 45);
  – EU money has helped improve roads, piers and ferries in areas like the Highlands (see p 47).

Perhaps Brussels is the capital of Scotland rather than Edinburgh (or is it London)?

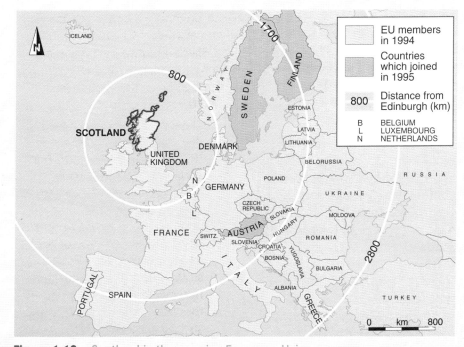

Figure 1.10   Scotland in the growing European Union

Scotland: Locations and Links

Size

Scotland is a small country, slightly smaller than Austria, but a little larger than the Irish Republic. Its area is 79 000 km² or just over half the size of England. Look at the scale on the maps. You will see that its length is much greater than its width, and that no place is very far from the sea.

Location

Figure 2.1 shows you how Scotland's position on the earth's surface can be located. This is done using latitude and longitude. Latitude is the distance from the equator, and longitude is distance from Greenwich in London. You should notice that all of Scotland lies west of Greenwich (longitude). Most of it is between 55° and 60° north of the equator (latitude). The map shows that the most northerly and easterly parts are both in the Shetland Islands. St Kilda is the most westerly point. The most southerly is the Mull of Galloway.

Results of location

- Because of differences in longitude, the sun rises about 30 minutes earlier in Shetland than in St Kilda.
- Because of differences in latitude, the Shetlands have one hour more daylight in summer (and one hour less in winter) than Galloway.

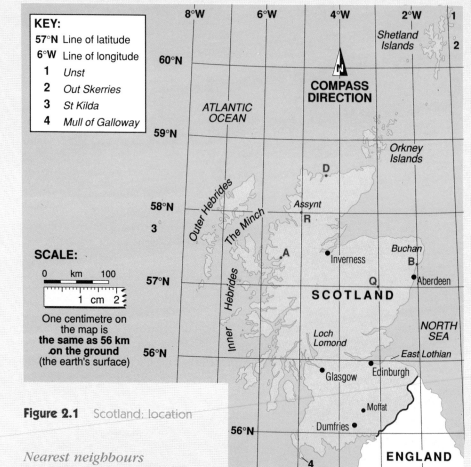

KEY:
57°N Line of latitude
6°W Line of longitude
1 Unst
2 Out Skerries
3 St Kilda
4 Mull of Galloway

SCALE:
0 km 100
1 cm 2
One centimetre on the map is **the same as 56 km on the ground** (the earth's surface)

Figure 2.1 Scotland: location

Nearest neighbours

Scotland has a land boundary with England. Ireland is only 20 km south west of the Mull of Kintyre. The Shetlands are much closer to Norway and the Faeroes than they are to London.

Links

Figure 2.2 shows that Scotland has ferry links with Ireland all year round. There are also summer services between Shetland, Norway and the Faeroes.
There are many important ferry services linking the mainland of Scotland with the inhabited islands off the north and west coasts. The ferries are expensive to run, and may be disrupted by gales. The ferries now carry more passengers and cars, and less freight, than before.
The map in Figure 2.2 also shows seaports and railways. The railway links used to be more extensive, despite the rugged landscape. More people own cars now, so there are fewer rail passengers. Coal mines and steelworks have closed down, so there is less freight for railways to carry. There are fears that more lines in the Highlands will close, despite their importance for tourism and for local people.

Roads and Bridges

Links by main road are much better than by rail in Scotland. Figure 2.3 shows that there are motorways in central Scotland. The M8 is the busiest road in Scotland, but most important links by road are from north to south, e.g. the A9. These roads follow major river valleys to cut through the hills and mountains. The flow of traffic through towns has been reduced by the building of bypasses, e.g. round Edinburgh.

The length of journeys has been reduced by the building of road bridges across firths. The first of these, and the busiest, was the Forth Road Bridge. Some experts now think there is a need for a second road bridge across the Firth of Forth. Another new road bridge has replaced the ferry from Kyle of Lochalsh to Skye. Figure 2.3 shows how the building of three bridges has shortened the route of the A9 north of Inverness.

Large areas of the country have few communication links. Few people live here, sometimes in a very rugged landscape like the North West Highlands. The island communities are linked to essential services in the largest cities by air routes, e.g. the service from Glasgow to Barra uses the beach as the runway.

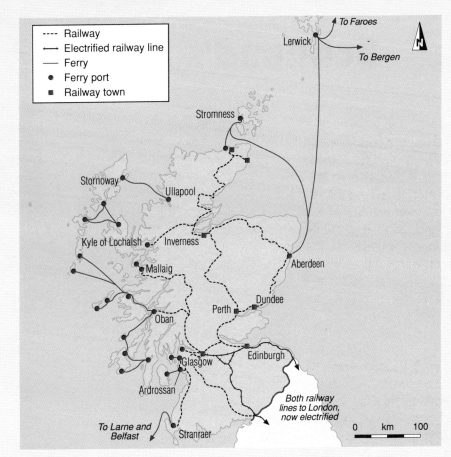

Figure 2.2 Railways and ferries

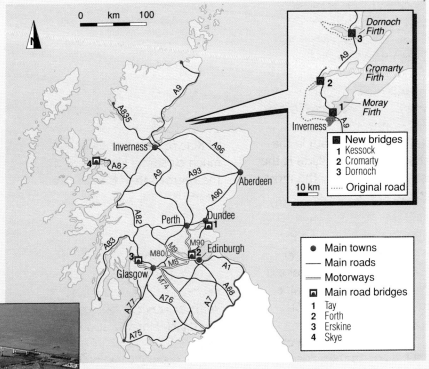

Figure 2.3 Main road links in mainland Scotland

Figure 2.4 Since the Kessock Bridge was built, journey times between the expanding villages in the Black Isle (background) and Inverness (foreground) have been shortened

Scotland's Rocks

3

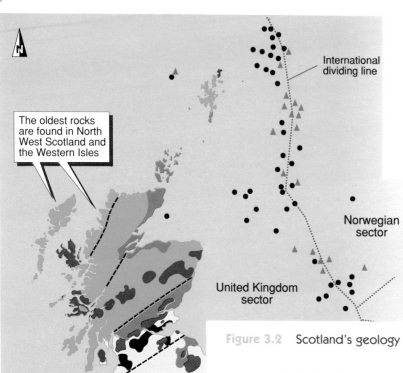

The oldest rocks are found in North West Scotland and the Western Isles

Figure 3.2 Scotland's geology

Figure 3.1 Suilven, near Lochinver

Igneous rocks
- Lavas
- Granite

Metamorphic rocks --- Fault lines

Sedimentary rocks ● Oilfield
- Coal ▲ Gasfield
- Old Red Sandstone
- Other sedimentary rock

There are hundreds of different kinds of rock in Scotland. They are an important part of the landscape, and have given us important resources from early times (Figure 3.6).

Rocks of the North West

Some of Scotland's rocks are among the oldest in the world. The rock forming the low ground in Figure 3.1 is around 2700 million years old. Suilven, the mountain, is not so old – only 800 million years! Like many mountains of north west Scotland, Suilven is all that is left of thick rock once deposited on top of the older rocks. The rest was eroded (worn away) by rivers and ice.

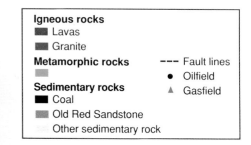

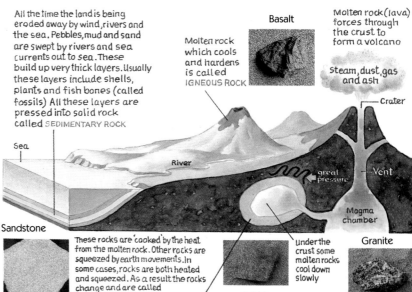

Figure 3.3 Types of rock

Past Volcanic Eruptions

Over millions of years rocks have formed in different ways. Figure 3.3 shows how this took place. Sometimes the earth moved violently. Lava flowed and ash was blasted high into the sky as new **volcanoes** formed. You can see active volcanoes in Figure 3.4. Today the Castle Rock and Arthur's Seat in Edinburgh, the Bass Rock, and North Berwick Law are just small parts of once large volcanoes. Thankfully they are long extinct.

Once there were Tropical Forests

About 330 million years ago, another type of rock began to form. The climate was hotter and wetter: parts of Scotland were covered with swamps, tropical trees and giant ferns. Huge dragonflies with wingspans up to 75 cm flew about (Figure 3.5). Eventually dead trees and plants fell into the swamps and were covered by sea and sand. The dead wood slowly hardened to form coal. This was how Scotland's coalfields developed (Figure 3.2).

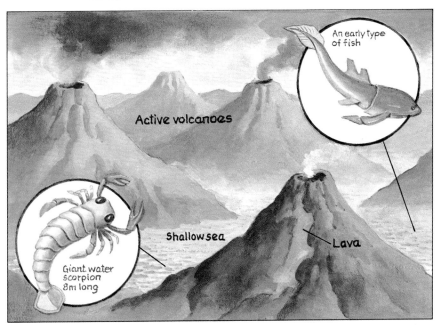

Figure 3.4 Volcanoes in Central Scotland (400 million years ago)

Figure 3.5 A coal swamp in Central Scotland (320 million years ago)

Rocks as Resources

Coal has been used in Scotland for some 800 years. It is just one of many rocks that have been mined, quarried and drilled to give us:

- building materials, e.g. stone, slate, gravel and cement
- energy, e.g. coal, natural gas and oil (Figure 3.2).

Nowadays we each consume 7 tonnes of rock a year! Some of these resources are exported, e.g. oil from under the North Sea, and building stone from a coastal 'super-quarry' at Glensanda on Loch Linnhe

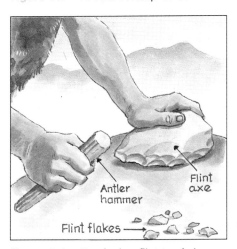

Figure 3.6 Producing flint tools in Buchan in prehistoric times

Figure 3.7 Visitors examining steeply sloping beds of Old Red Sandstone in Berwickshire

Figure 3.8 A primary school in Peebles built of Old Red Sandstone at the beginning of the twentieth century

Ice-Age Scotland

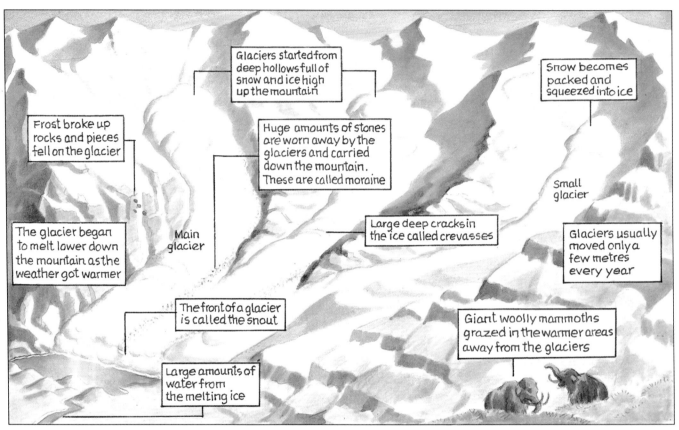

Figure 4.1   Mountains in Ice-Age Scotland

Labels within Figure 4.1:

- Glaciers started from deep hollows full of snow and ice high up the mountain
- Snow becomes packed and squeezed into ice
- Frost broke up rocks and pieces fell on the glacier
- Huge amounts of stones are worn away by the glaciers and carried down the mountain. These are called moraine
- Small glacier
- The glacier began to melt lower down the mountain as the weather got warmer
- Main glacier
- Large deep cracks in the ice called crevasses
- Glaciers usually moved only a few metres every year
- The front of a glacier is called the snout
- Giant woolly mammoths grazed in the warmer areas away from the glaciers
- Large amounts of water from the melting ice

Scotland was once covered with ice. In fact, during the **Ice Age**, most of the British Isles lay under ice, often hundreds of metres thick. Heavy snow fell in the mountains. Layers of snow built up in the high hollows. Gradually this snow was squeezed into ice. Very slowly, once the hollows were full, some of the ice crept down from the mountains into the valleys below. These slow-moving 'rivers of ice' are called glaciers; they have helped to shape Scotland's hills, mountains, lochs and lowlands. The sketch in Figure 4.1 shows how the Scottish mountains might have looked during the last Ice Age.

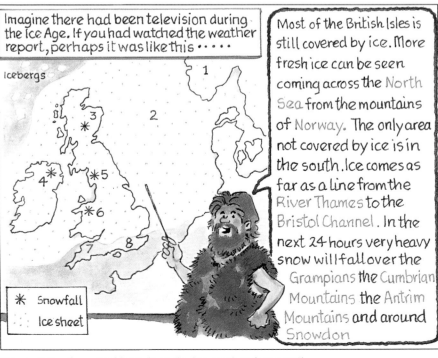

Imagine there had been television during the Ice Age. If you had watched the weather report, perhaps it was like this • • • •

Icebergs

* Snowfall
∴ Ice sheet

Most of the British Isles is still covered by ice. More fresh ice can be seen coming across the North Sea from the mountains of Norway. The only area not covered by ice is in the south. Ice comes as far as a line from the River Thames to the Bristol Channel. In the next 24 hours very heavy snow will fall over the Grampians the Cumbrian Mountains the Antrim Mountains and around Snowdon

Figure 4.2   '. . . And here is today's weather forecast!'

After the Ice Age: in the Mountains

Once the ice had all melted, the mountains looked different. Large, deep hollows were now left high on the mountainsides where the glaciers had begun. In Scotland, these hollows are called corries. Sometimes there is a loch at the bottom of the corrie, as in Figure 4.3. Where there had been a shallow river valley, there were now deep, steep-sided valleys with level floors. The glacier had acted like a giant file grinding away at the land, and shaping valleys like that in Figure 4.4. There were sometimes lochs there, long and narrow like Loch Avon in Figure 4.4. Scotland's largest lochs – Lomond, Ness, Tay – occupy similar deep glaciated valleys.

Figure 4.3
Farquhar's Corrie, Beinn Eigh, is one of the most impressive corries in the Highlands. Can you see the loch, the 400 m high cliffs and the different coloured rocks?

Figure 4.4
Loch Avon far below the plateau of the Cairngorms. Can you make out the deep U-shaped valley?

Figure 4.5 A drumlin, a low hill shaped like an upturned boat, overlooks the former distillery at Bladnoch, Dumfries & Galloway

After the Ice Age: in the Lowlands

Most of the soil and stone was eroded from the mountains and dropped in the lowlands. But, at times, the thick ice had broken up the lowland rocks as well. As a result, many of Scotland's lowlands are plastered over by thick deposits. This mixture of soil and stone is called glacial till. It often gives fertile soil for farming.

Sometimes, as in Figure 4.5, such deposits have been shaped by the ice into smooth, rounded hillocks. If you visit the centre of Glasgow, it is built on similar small hills, called **drumlins**. Figure 4.6 shows how glaciers have also helped shape the centre of Edinburgh.

Remains of Arthur's Seat volcano

Old Edinburgh grew up on the tail of softer rock

Steep west facing slope of volcanic crag

Direction of ice sheet

Figure 4.6 The Old Town of Edinburgh

Highlands and Lowlands

Scotland is one of the more stable parts of the earth's surface. But some places, e.g. Crieff, still have earth tremors. This is because Crieff sits on top of one of the major **fault lines** in the country. It runs between Helensburgh and Stonehaven (see Figure 5.1). Such tremors are recorded on the **seismograph** in the Royal Observatory, Blackford Hill, Edinburgh. But they are very low on the Richter Scale, and do not do any damage. There must have been violent earthquakes in the past. Look at Figure 5.1 again. Notice the other major fault lines, which also run from south west to north east. Sometime in the past, as a result of catastrophic earthquakes over many years, all the land between two of these parallel faults sank downwards. The scars on the landscape have long since healed, but there are still very steep slopes along the fault lines. These mark the boundaries which separate Central Scotland (or the Midland Valley) from the two upland areas on either side. These are:

- the Southern Uplands, where the highest summits rise just over 840 m;
- the Scottish Highlands, where there are many summits over 1000 m. Another fault line along the Great Glen divides the Highlands into the Grampian Highlands and the North West Highlands.

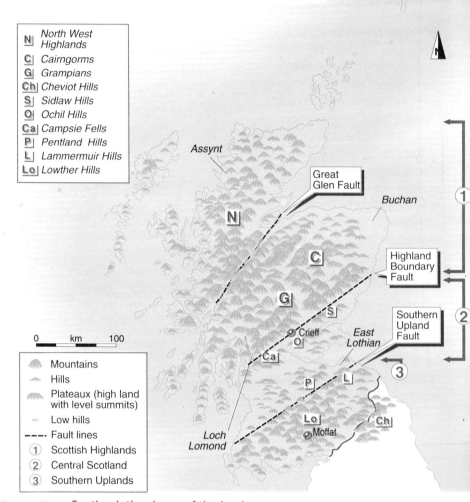

N	North West Highlands
C	Cairngorms
G	Grampians
Ch	Cheviot Hills
S	Sidlaw Hills
O	Ochil Hills
Ca	Campsie Fells
P	Pentland Hills
L	Lammermuir Hills
Lo	Lowther Hills

Mountains
Hills
Plateaux (high land with level summits)
Low hills
- - - - Fault lines
1 Scottish Highlands
2 Central Scotland
3 Southern Uplands

Figure 5.1   Scotland: the shape of the land

Most of the summits in Scotland are smooth and rounded. The jagged peaks of the Cuillins in Skye are very unusual (see Figure 5.3).

Sometimes the land between the two faults is called the Central Lowlands. This is misleading, because Central Scotland contains **ridges** and **plateaux** of higher ground, e.g. the Ochil Hills reach 721 m (see Figure 5.5). These higher areas are made of igneous rock. However, there are large lowland areas of sedimentary rock as Figure 3.2 on p 8 shows. About half of Scotland is less than 185 m above sea level, but very little of this is a completely flat **plain**. The Carse of Gowrie and the Carse of Stirling are rare examples of plains. Most of Scotland consists of hills, plateaux, and mountains. River valleys provide lower ground in such areas. Broad deep valleys are known as *dales* in the Southern Uplands and *straths* in the Highlands. *Glens* are very narrow, deep valleys in the Highlands.

The west coast of Scotland rises steeply from the sea except in Ayrshire, in Central Scotland. The east coast of Scotland has most of the lowland areas. These are also the best farming areas, since they are the driest and sunniest (see pages 21 and 24).

Land above 360 m
Land between 120 and 360 m
Land from sea level to 120 m

▲ Summits over 900 m

△ Other summits

Cairngorm Plateau

0   km   100

460 m △

479 m △

Caithness

Foinavon
908 m

Suilven 737 m

Laigh of
Moray

799 m △

Ben Eighe
1010 m

Buchan
Plateau

Glen More

Strathspey

Cairngorm 1245 m
Ben Macdui 1309 m
Lochnagar 1155 m

Cuillin Hills
1009 m

Ben Nevis
1343 m

Cruachan
1124 m

Strathmore

Carse of Gowrie
Strathearn
Howe of Fife

en Lawers
1214 m

Ben More
966 m

Carse of Stirling

Middle Clyde
Valley

Lothian

The Merse

Goat Fell
874 m

Tinto △
712 m

Broad Law 840 m

Ayrshire

Merrick
842 m

Criffel △
569 m

Annandale
Nithsdale

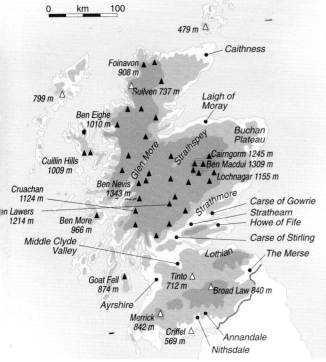

Scotland: highland and lowland

Figure 5.3   The unusual jagged summits of the Cuillins attract many climbers. Try to show the peaks, the steep slopes and the loch in a sketch

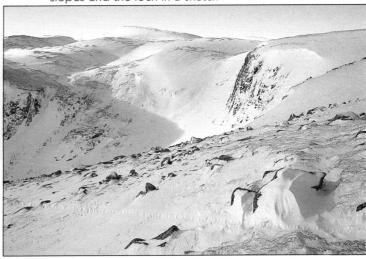

Figure 5.4   The Cairngorms, which are the most extensive area of high ground in Scotland, have a plateau summit about 1200 m

Figure 5.5   The Ochil Hills drop very steeply along a fault line to the flat carse lands near Stirling

Figure 5.6   b) The almost level land in lower Nithsdale, south west Scotland, provides rich pastures

a) Fertile farmland in the rolling drumlin landscape of the Merse, south east Scotland

Contrasting Landscapes

Three examples of Scotland's landscapes are shown in Figures 6.1–6.6. Each landscape is distinct, with different locations, types of rock, climate and land use.

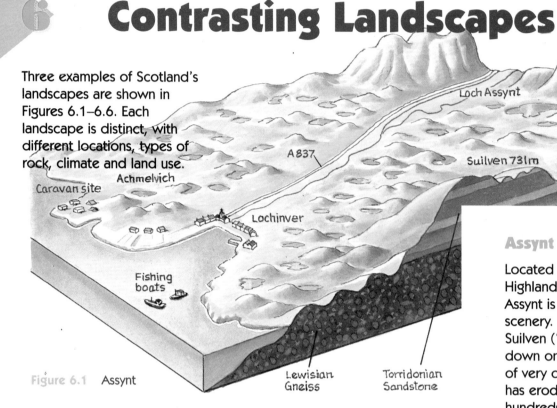

Figure 6.1   Assynt

Assynt

Located in the North West Highlands, the district of Assynt is famous for its scenery. Bold mountains like Suilven ('pillar mountain') look down on bumpy, lower land of very old, hard rocks. Ice has eroded this area and left hundreds of lochs, large and small. Although remote, Assynt attracts tourists. About 70 per cent of them come from abroad to enjoy the scenery, walk, climb, fish, and visit the occasional sandy beach, e.g. at Achmelvich. Most of the people live around the coast in crofting 'townships' and in Lochinver, the main village, fishing is important. Most of the trawlers are from north east Scotland, and have been joined recently by French vessels.

Figure 6.2   The area around Lochinver. You should be able to pick out the two mountains of Canisp and Suilven overlooking the village of Lochinver

East Lothian Coastlands

The part of East Lothian shown in Figure 6.6 is warmer, drier, and less windy than Assynt. With level land and fertile soil, this is one of the main **arable** (crop) **farming** areas of Scotland. There are several steep-sided hills. Although not very high, North Berwick Law, the Garleton Hills and the offshore Bass Rock are all that remain of large volcanoes, active millions of years ago. East Lothian is popular: there are beaches, golf courses, attractive villages, and towns. Many people have moved to resorts like North Berwick or villages like Athelstaneford, and travel to work in Edinburgh by road or rail.

Figure 6.3   East Lothian: arable fields on level land with the cone-shaped North Berwick Law and Firth of Forth beyond

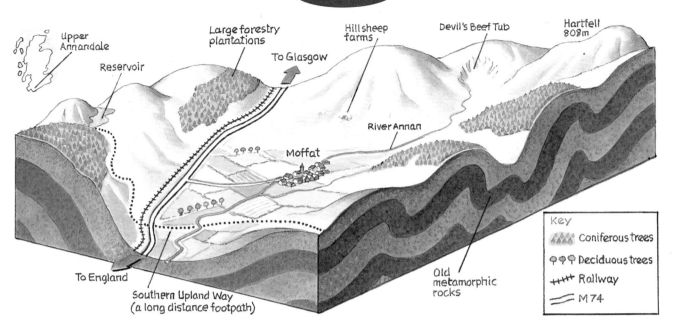

Figure 6.4   Upper Annandale

Upper Annandale

The hills shown in Figures 6.4 and 6.5 are part of the Southern Uplands. Their summits were once much higher, but they have been worn down and now have a rounded shape. Glaciers helped to deepen valleys like Moffatdale and Annandale, and to erode the deep hollow called the Devil's Beef Tub. (Rustled cattle were once hidden here by the Border reivers). Here the River Annan has its source. As it flows south, its valley is followed by the main road (the M74) and railway line to England. The steep slope, thin soils and heavy rain suit sheep farming, forestry and water supply. Like the two other areas, it is popular with tourists. A few of the more active may walk the Southern Upland Way. Many come in bus parties to the small town of Moffat, with its gift shops (selling Moffat toffee among other things) and hotels.

Figure 6.5   Annandale near Moffat. You should see clearly the difference between the improved farmland and the moorland

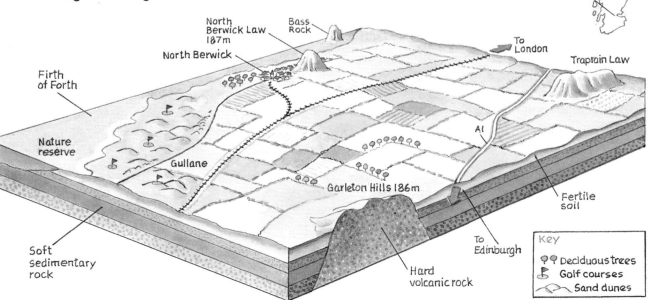

Figure 6.6   East Lothian

Scotland's Coastline

Figure 7.1   Loch Leven in Argyll is a good example of a west coast sea loch

Figure 7.2   Brightly coloured with flowers in spring, the machair provides good grazing

▲▲▲ Important cliffs
     Important beaches
✳ Possible super-quarry

1 Dornoch Firth
2 Cromarty Firth
3 Firth of Lorne
4 Firth of Clyde

0   km   100

St Ninian's Isle

Old Man of Hoy
Cape Wrath
Butt of Lewis
Pentland Firth
Moray Firth
Lingarabay ✳

The west coast has many long narrow sea lochs with islands offshore

Loch Leven

Firth of Tay
Firth of Forth

Solway Firth

There are several wide open bays in South West Scotland

The east coast has only five main inlets and the surrounding land is much lower than the west coast

Figure 7.3   Scotland's coastline

West/East Differences

For its size, Scotland has a very long coastline. If you straightened out all the bends and twists, you would have a line about 10 000 km long. Looking at the map in Figure 7.3, you can see that the west coast has many more inlets, sea lochs, and islands than the east. Fig 7.1 shows one of these sea lochs – Loch Leven. Notice the steep-sided mountains and how far the sea stretches inland.

Beaches, Spits and Tombolos

Figure 7.3 shows many beaches around the coast. In the Outer Hebrides, there are many kilometres of beautiful beach. Behind them are grass-covered sandy areas called the machair (Figure 7.2) which are rich in wild flowers in early summer. Beaches change shape as the tides move sand from place to place.
Sometimes a **spit** forms – a long finger of sand that grows out to sea. When a spit joins on to a nearby island it forms a **tombolo**, as shown in Figure 7.4 of St Ninian's Isle.

Figure 7.4   The sandy tombolo joining St Ninian's Isle to the Shetland mainland

Cliffs and Stacks

Scotland has some very spectacular cliffs. On Orkney and Shetland they are up to 300 m high. But cliffs, like beaches, can change shape. High winds and stormy conditions cause large waves, which throw loose rocks at the cliffs. Cracks open up, caves form and may erode even more to become an arch. When an arch collapses, a pillar or stack is left. The Old Man of Hoy (Figure 7.5) is perhaps the best known in Scotland.

Figure 7.5   The Old Man of Hoy in Orkney. Can you see the red sandstone stack, the vertical cliff and the Pentland Firth?

People and the Coastline

Not all of Scotland's coastline is as beautiful or as empty as the areas shown in Figures 7.1 and 7.4. There are many places where the coast has been built on or changed by people. Figure 7.6 shows some of the ways in which the coastline may be used. On the right-hand side, you can see such things as docks, factories, and power stations. On the left-hand side, you can see how the coast may be used by holiday-makers or anyone wishing to enjoy the open air, scenery or wildlife.

Figure 7.6 also shows some of the ways in which we spoil our coastline. People have different ideas about using the coast. On Harris in the Western Isles, for example, there were arguments for and against a plan for a very large super-quarry at Lingarabay. This was an example of **land use conflict**.

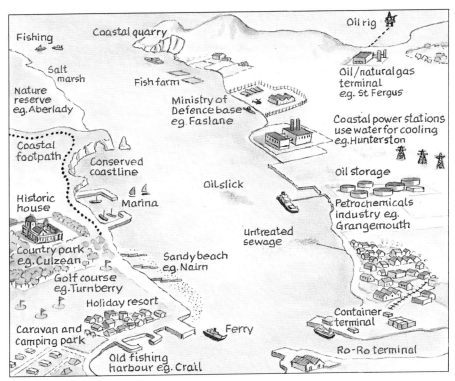

Figure 7.6   Using and abusing Scotland's coastline

Figure 7.7   Lingarabay, Harris. Much of the hill above the bay would be excavated in the proposed super-quarry

Redland, a large building firm, plan to remove 600 million tonnes of hard igneous rock. When they finish, after 60 to 100 years, the quarry will be flooded. A hill will have become a sea loch

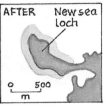

We want to dig the biggest quarry in Europe. Ships will take away millions of tonnes of rock. It's hard rock-ideal for building roads. People in England, Europe and the USA need more rock every year. We'll give you jobs and put money into the area. Remember, if there's a problem, we can always go to Norway or Spain instead
Company Representative

This quarry will spoil the scenery, there will be a lot of noise and dust. Don't they know that the tourists-our guests-come here for the peace and quiet?
Hotel Owner

I hope the firm comes. Maybe I'll get a job. They've promised up to 90 jobs, and that's a lot for this place. I would not need to leave the island then
School Leaver

The local churches welcome the new jobs. But we are worried that there will be work on Sunday at the quarry. In Harris, we believe that Sunday is a day for rest and going to church, not for work
Local Minister

I've lived here all my life. I work the land and I do a bit of fishing. We need the quarry, but the ships bother me. They'll bring ballast water from goodness knows where. They'll dump it before they load the rocks. The dumped water will pollute the local sea water. Fish and fish farms will be affected
Crofter

Scotland's Coastline

Rivers, Lochs and Water Supply

Scotland has many rivers and lochs because of the high rainfall in the mountains and hills where the rivers have their sources. Figure 8.1 shows some of the main rivers and fresh water lochs. Most of the rivers shown flow east into the North Sea or south into the Solway Firth. They tend to be longer and to flow more slowly than those which flow west into the Atlantic Ocean. The longest river is the Tay (188 km). Many rivers in the Highlands flow through long, deep and narrow lochs such as Loch Lomond, Loch Tay and Loch Earn. There is a string of three lochs along the Great Glen.

Rivers

As rivers flow from source to mouth, where they enter the sea, they gradually change. Not all rivers change in exactly the same way, but all are joined by smaller streams or tributaries. In general, rivers and their valleys change in the following ways:

- the width and depth of the river increases;
- the speed of the river decreases;
- the volume of water increases;
- the valley widens and the land becomes flatter.

The map of the River Nith (Figure 8.2) shows the changes in one particular river.

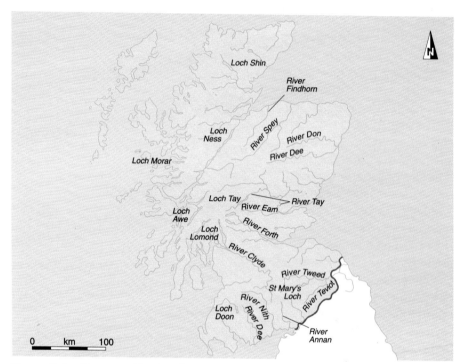

Figure 8.1   Rivers and lochs of mainland Scotland

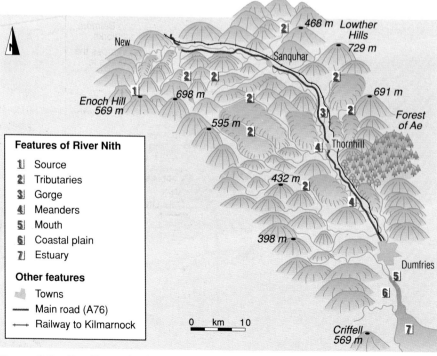

Figure 8.2   The River Nith (see Figure 5.6b)

Rivers and People

Rivers and their valleys are important to people in different ways:

- rivers provided water, fish and power as well as a means of transport in past times;
- rivers often flood low land;
- river valleys provide routeways through hills and mountains;
- river valleys provide better farmland in mountains and hilly country;
- rivers may have to be bridged to avoid long **detours**;
- settlements, mills and power stations may be built on river banks;
- rivers may become polluted because of this.

The diagram in Figure 8.3 show how the River Dee, at Tongland in Galloway, has affected people.

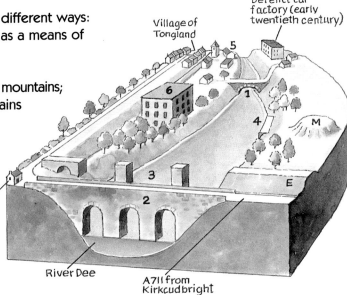

Key

1 Old stone bridge built in 1765
2 Toll bridge built by Telford in 1805
3 Support of dismantled railway bridge (1850–1965)
4 Site of quay from which ships carried catches of salmon to London
5 Old water mills in Tongland

6 Tongland hydro-electric power station built in 1933. The water is brought through a pipe from the dam 500 m upstream
E Former railway embankment
M Site of Motte and Bailey castle

Figure 8.3   The River Dee at Tongland, Galloway

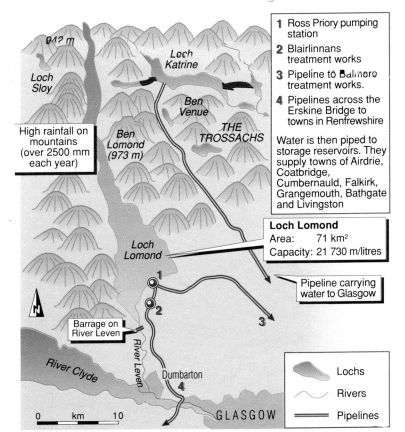

1 Ross Priory pumping station
2 Blairlinnans treatment works
3 Pipeline to Balmore treatment works.
4 Pipelines across the Erskine Bridge to towns in Renfrewshire

Water is then piped to storage reservoirs. They supply towns of Airdrie, Coatbridge, Cumbernauld, Falkirk, Grangemouth, Bathgate and Livingston

Loch Lomond
Area: 71 km²
Capacity: 21 730 m/litres

Pipeline carrying water to Glasgow

Lochs
Rivers
Pipelines

Figure 8.4   Water supply for the towns: Loch Lomond

Floods

Many river valleys are often still affected by floods. The flood waters deposit new soil on the farmland, and cause great damage.

Lochs and People

Scottish lochs are attractive to tourists in different ways. Some come to admire the scenery. Anglers come to fish for salmon and trout. Others use the lochs for water sports. Some lochs are important sources of water.

In 1859, Glasgow became the first town in Scotland to have a public supply of clean water. The water came from Loch Katrine in the Trossachs. This was close to the city, in an area of high rainfall. Figure 8.4 shows how the water is collected. Today, Loch Lomond not only supplies the Glasgow area, but towns as far away as Livingston.

Water has to be purified before it can be used. Now the big rivers (Clyde, Forth, Tweed) have river purification boards, which try to solve the river pollution problems.

9 Scotland's Climate

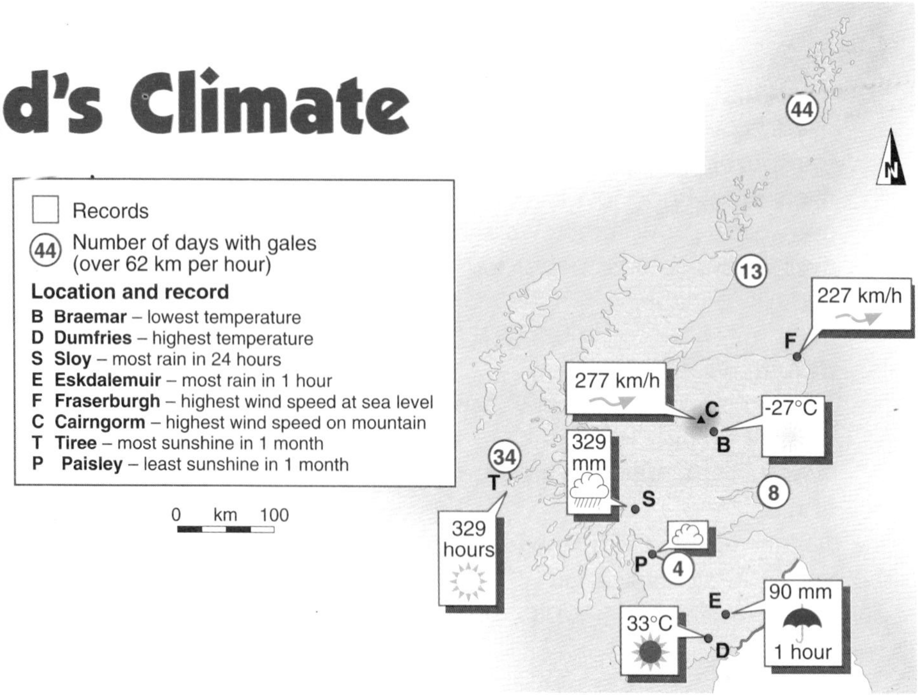
Records
44 Number of days with gales (over 62 km per hour)
Location and record
B Braemar – lowest temperature
D Dumfries – highest temperature
S Sloy – most rain in 24 hours
E Eskdalemuir – most rain in 1 hour
F Fraserburgh – highest wind speed at sea level
C Cairngorm – highest wind speed on mountain
T Tiree – most sunshine in 1 month
P Paisley – least sunshine in 1 month
0 km 100
44
13
227 km/h
F
277 km/h
C
-27°C
B
34
T
329 mm
S
8
329 hours
P
4
E
90 mm
1 hour
33°C
D

Figure 9.1 Records and gales

Scotland's Weather Records

Did you know?

- Scotland's hottest place ever has been Dumfries.
- The coolest place ever has been Braemar.
- The wettest places have been Sloy and Eskdalemuir.
- The sunniest has been Tiree.
- The cloudiest has been Paisley.
- The windiest have been Fraserburgh and Cairngorm.

These were extreme occasions, but they tell us something about Scotland's climate.

- In summer, places in the south are warmer than places in the north.
- In winter, the coldest places are in deep valleys in the Scottish Highlands.
- The wettest places are in highland areas near the west coast.
- The windiest places are at the coast or on mountain tops.

The facts about sunshine and cloud are not quite so helpful. However, it is true to say that low-lying areas near the coasts, both east and west, are the sunniest parts of Scotland.

Weather and Climate

The records above are for individual days or months. That is, they tell us about our **weather**. Our weather is usually very changeable. The word used to describe average, daily weather conditions is **climate**

Despite what people say, the Scottish climate is moderate, or temperate. That means that there is not much difference between winter and summer. The extremes listed at the top of this page are unusual. Compared to many other countries, Scotland has mild wet winters, and cool cloudy summers.

Rainfall in Scotland

There is rarely a shortage of rain (a **drought**). Figure 9.2 tells us the following.

- About one-third of the country is very wet. These areas are the mountains and hills in the west. These are the cloudiest areas.
- About one-sixth of the country does not have much rainfall (less than 750 mm per year). These drier areas are the lowlands near the east coast. Sheltered by the wet mountainous and hilly areas to the west, they are in a **rain shadow**. Look at Figure 9.4 opposite. They are among the sunniest areas of Scotland.

Most of the rain in Scotland is brought by warm, moist air coming in from the Atlantic Ocean.

Temperatures

Look at Figure 9.3. Because Scotland is such a small country, temperatures do not vary a great deal. However, on average:

- it gets colder as height increases;
- coastal areas are cooler in summer and warmer in winter than inland areas;
- the south of Scotland is warmer than the north in summer;
- the west of Scotland is warmer than the east in winter.

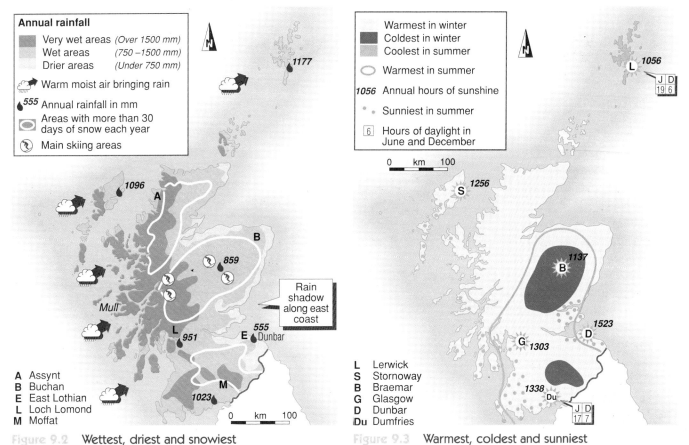

Annual rainfall

■ Very wet areas (Over 1500 mm)
■ Wet areas (750 –1500 mm)
□ Drier areas (Under 750 mm)

🌧 Warm moist air bringing rain

💧555 Annual rainfall in mm

⬭ Areas with more than 30 days of snow each year

🎿 Main skiing areas

A Assynt
B Buchan
E East Lothian
L Loch Lomond
M Moffat

1096
1177
1096
859
951
555 Dunbar
1023

Rain shadow along east coast

Mull

Figure 9.2 Wettest, driest and snowiest

Warmest in winter
Coldest in winter
Coolest in summer

⬭ Warmest in summer

1056 Annual hours of sunshine

· Sunniest in summer

6 Hours of daylight in June and December

L Lerwick
S Stornoway
B Braemar
G Glasgow
D Dunbar
Du Dumfries

L 1056 J D 19 6
S 1256
B 1137
1523
G 1303
D
1338
Du J D 17 7

0 km 100

Figure 9.3 Warmest, coldest and sunniest

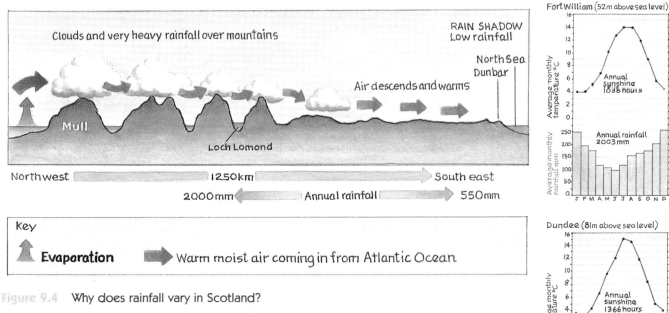

Clouds and very heavy rainfall over mountains

RAIN SHADOW Low rainfall

North Sea
Dunbar

Air descends and warms

Mull

Loch Lomond

Northwest ▭ 1250km ▭ South east

2000mm ◄ Annual rainfall ► 550mm

Key

⬆ **Evaporation**   ➡ Warm moist air coming in from Atlantic Ocean

Figure 9.4 Why does rainfall vary in Scotland?

West/East Contrasts

Look at the climate graphs for Fort William and Dundee in Figure 9.5. They show the differences between the west and the east of Scotland. In particular, they show that Dundee is in the rain shadow on the east coast. The diagram in Figure 9.4 shows why there is a rain shadow. Dunbar is even drier than Dundee.

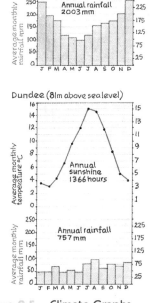

Fort William (52m above sea level)

Annual sunshine 1058 hours

Annual rainfall 2003 mm

Dundee (81m above sea level)

Annual sunshine 1366 hours

Annual rainfall 757 mm

Figure 9.5 Climate Graphs

10 Weather and People

Weather in Towns

People living in large built-up areas are sometimes less aware of the weather. Their houses may have central heating and double glazing. Others may be very aware of cold, dampness, and gale force winds if their houses are sub-standard.

Large settlements create their own modified climate. Figure 10.1 shows how buildings, e.g. in Central Glasgow or Edinburgh, give off heat, create shadows, and funnel winds.

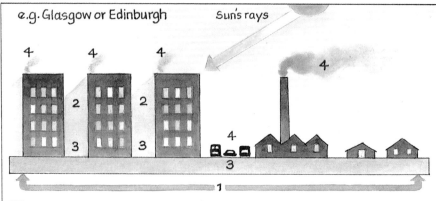

Key
1 Large concentrations of buildings give out heat and raise winter temperatures
2 Tall buildings prevent sunshine from reaching street level, especially in winter
3 Winds increase in force through narrow streets
4 Fumes from chimneys, vents and vehicle exhausts can cause haze or fog
5 Winter snow and ice can cause traffic problems

Figure 10.1   Weather in towns

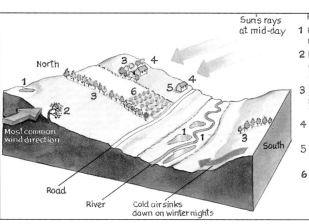

Key
1 Flat land flooded by heavy rain and melting snow
2 Prevailing winds bend trees and force them to grow in a twisted shape
3 Farmers plant trees to shelter animals, crops and houses from the prevailing wind
4 Houses are built and crops planted facing the sun
5 Gable end of houses face the prevailing wind
6 Soft fruits and orchards on hill slope above frosty valley floor. In winter, the countryside is colder than towns

Figure 10.2   Weather in the Scottish countryside

Weather in the Countryside

The weather is much more important to people who live and work in the countryside (Figure 10.2). They have to be careful about the position of their houses in relation to:
- exposure to the sun;
- exposure to the wind;
- possible flood danger.

The work they do is always affected by the weather. The following descriptions were written by a shepherd on a hill farm in the mountains east of Loch Lomond.

Winter

'January is usually the wettest month of the year, but this year, instead of rain we have snow . . . with night temperatures of –24°C. The blizzard struck without warning from the north . . .'

Spring

'The cruel east wind mercifully veers to the south west. Warmth returns to the sun . . . lovely green grass is growing up in the sheltered sun traps . . .'

Autumn

'Sharp nights and misty mornings are commonplace . . . It starts to rain. And how it rains . . . the Strone Burn boils out white far into the dark, storm-lashed loch.'

Red Skye at Night, J Barrington

Figure 10.3   Tourists in the Royal Mile on a rainy day in August, usually Edinburgh's wettest month of the year

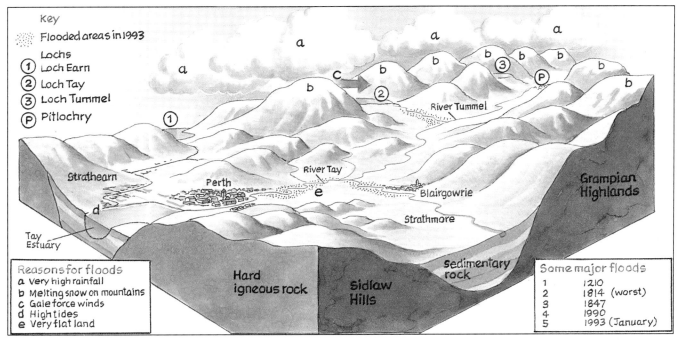

Key
~ Flooded areas in 1993
  Lochs
① Loch Earn
② Loch Tay
③ Loch Tummel
Ⓟ Pitlochry

Reasons for floods
a Very high rainfall
b Melting snow on mountains
c Gale force winds
d High tides
e Very flat land

Some major floods
1   1210
2   1814 (worst)
3   1847
4   1990
5   1993 (January)

Figure 10.4   Floods along the River Tay

The River Tay is Scotland's longest and most important river. Its source is in the Grampian Highlands. It flows through the very long and narrow Loch Tay. It has many important tributaries such as the Rivers Tummel, Garry, Earn, Ericht, and Isla. Why is it important?
– It is famous for its salmon fishing (Figure 10.5).
– The scenery of river, lochs and mountains attracts many tourists.
– The valleys of the Tay and its tributaries provide routeways through the mountains. The A9 and the Edinburgh/Inverness railway follow the valleys of the Tay, the Tummel, and the Garry.
– There is rich farmland on the valley floor.
– There are **hydro-electric power** stations on the Tummel and the Garry.
– Many people live in towns (such as Perth) and villages on the valley floor.

However, living near the River Tay can be dangerous. The level valley floor is often flooded, e.g. in 1990 and 1993. The block diagram in Figure 10.4 suggests reasons for these floods. In 1993, the river rose 3.6 m above normal level. Many houses in Perth were affected. Elsewhere, bridges were destroyed and farmland damaged as the photograph in Figure 10.6 shows.

Figure 10.5   Salmon fishing with rod and line is an important and sometimes expensive recreation on the River Tay

Figure 10.6   Notice the depth of the flood water on the valley floor of the River Tay

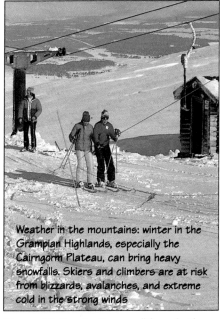

Weather in the mountains: winter in the Grampian Highlands, especially the Cairngorm Plateau, can bring heavy snowfalls. Skiers and climbers are at risk from blizzards, avalanches, and extreme cold in the strong winds

Figure 10.7   Arctic conditions in the Cairngorms can be dangerous but the snow attracts skiers

11 Scotland: Farming

Look at the map in Figure 11.2 of types of farming in Scotland. The key to the map is given in detail below.

Types of Farming: Key

1 In these most difficult farming areas, there are large hill sheep farms. Almost all the land is covered in rough grazing (coarse grasses and heather).

2 In these lower hill areas, the farms are smaller. Most of the land is still unimproved. The farmers raise beef cattle as well as sheep.

3 In these lowland areas of north east Scotland, beef cattle and sheep are reared and fattened. Most of the land is improved. Some farms grow potatoes for seed. Others specialise in rearing pigs and poultry. There are dairy farms near Aberdeen.

4 In these lowland areas of eastern Scotland, the farms specialise in growing crops. These include seed potatoes and soft fruits. There are some small market gardens growing vegetables. The land is level, the soil is fertile, and the rainfall is low. There are also pig and poultry farms. Dairy farms are found near the towns and cities.

5 In these lowland areas of western Scotland, the high rainfall helps grass to grow well. Farms specialise in producing milk from herds of dairy cattle. There are market gardens in the Clyde Valley and in Ayrshire. Early potatoes are grown in sandy soils.

6 In these scattered lowland areas on the edge of the North West Highlands and the Islands, there are tiny part-time farms called crofts.

Most of Scotland (areas 1, 2, 3 and 6 on Figure 11.2) is described as 'least-favoured'. Farmers in these areas are helped by extra payments from the European Union.

Figure 11.1 Looking south to Black Hill in the Pentland Hills with improved pasture in the foreground and heather moor on the hills

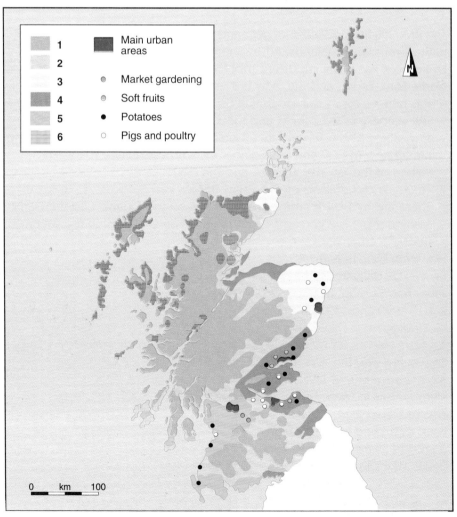

Figure 11.2 Types of farming

Figure 11.3 Friesian dairy cattle on Langhill Farm, a dairy farm owned by Edinburgh University south of the city

Figure 11.4 · Raspberry harvest near Forfar in Strathmore, an area famous for its soft fruits

Figure 11.5 Aberdeen Angus beef cattle on improved pasture just above Flanders Moss between Aberfoyle and Stirling

How a farm Works

A Farm System

Farms are businesses in which the farmer tries to make a decent living. Crofters, for example, have to find other work to help keep them going. In bad years, some farmers make very little profit. All farmers rely on payments called subsidies from the government and the European Union. They also borrow money from the banks. As you will see later, farmers may now use their land in many ways to increase their income.

The diagram in Figure 11.6 shows how a farm business can be divided into three parts.

- What is put into the business by the farmer, his workers, and the land itself.
- What happens on the farm (crops grown, livestock reared or fattened).
- What the farm produces for sale.

These are usually called *inputs*, *processes*, and *outputs*. Together they make what is called a *system*. The example in 11.6 is for a very large sheep farm in Perthshire. Information about any farm in Scotland could be arranged in this way. You will find descriptions of three sample farms in Scotland on the following pages.

This is a very large farm of 4000 hectares on very difficult land in a very deep valley, ranging in height from 150 to 1150 metres. The rainfall is over 2500mm each year

INPUTS

1 The land
High, steep with thin soil (acid and stony)

2 Climate
Very wet all year; river liable to flood; frost and snow in winter

3 Grazing
Coarse grasses, heather and bracken

5 Money
Income from sales. Loans from banks. Subsidies from the government and the European Union. This is spent on wages, repairs, winter feed, vet fees, transport, renting winter grazing on lowland farms, new stock, taxes, insurance and repaying the bank loan

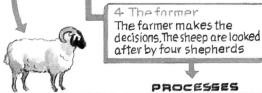

4 The farmer
The farmer makes the decisions. The sheep are looked after by four shepherds

PROCESSES

1 Sheep
3500 Blackface ewes are kept. In winter, one third are sent to graze on lowland farms on the Laigh of Moray

2 Cattle
80 beef cattle graze on the lower land. They are a mixture of Highland, Aberdeen Angus, Hereford and Luing breeds

3 Wildlife
The farmer rents out the shooting rights on the mountainsides. Wealthy visitors shoot red deer and grouse

OUTPUTS

1 Sheep
About 3000 lambs are sold each year plus surplus ewes and rams, Wool clip

2 Cattle
Sold to lowland farmers for fattening

3 Shooting
Venison and grouse are sold

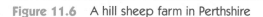

Figure 11.6 A hill sheep farm in Perthshire

12 Changing Farmscapes

Scotland's farming landscapes are changing rapidly. So too are the ways the land is farmed. Sometimes this is because the farmer decides to make changes to make more money. Often it is because the farmer has to obey new regulations from the British Government or the European Union.

The block diagrams in Figure 12.1 try to show some of the ways in which a lowland farming area might have changed in the last 25 years. In 1970, the farmscape was one which had been shaped by the eighteenth century **Agricultural Revolution**. The land was divided into medium-sized fields, separated by hedges and lines of trees. Farmers grew traditional crops and kept British breeds of livestock. By 1995, as the second diagram in Figure 12.1 shows, the farmscape had much changed. Ways of farming had also changed, and farmers had many new sources of income. Some farms had been completely transformed, as the following examples show.

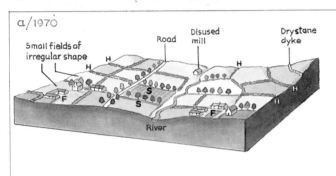

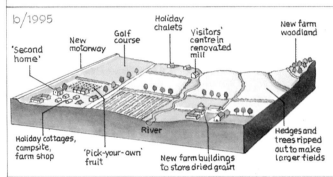

Figure 12.1   Changing farmscapes

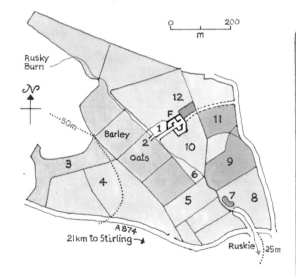

Figure 12.2   Dunaverig Farm

Key

1   Car park
2   Bridge over burn
3   Coppiced woodland
4   Ewes and lambs
5   Sheep and horses
6   Wildflower area
7   Mill pond
8   Jacob sheep
9   Strawberries and raspberries
10 Highland cattle
11 Other soft fruit
12 Orchard
F   Farm buildings, house, museum and tearoom

Dunaverig Farm

Dunaverig is a small farm of 32 ha near the Trossachs (see Figure 12.4). It is now run by the Stewart family as a farm museum and educational centre. The farm was too small to make money. The herd of 20 Ayrshire dairy cattle and the flock of 100 Greyface ewes were sold, and most of the land is now rented to neighbouring farmers.

The Stewarts have always been interested in the conservation of the countryside, e.g. building drystane dykes and coppicing woodland. Visitors can see these on the farm trail, visit the farm museum, or pick their own soft fruit.

'Sympathetic' Farming

Mr Mitchell is the farmer at Eaglescairnie Farm, a mixed farm of 152 ha near Gifford in East Lothian (see Figure 12.5). Figure 12.3 shows some of the ways in which he has made his farm more sympathetic to wildlife and improved the farmscape.

Figure 12.4 A major feature on Dunaverig Farm are the recently built or restored drystane dykes

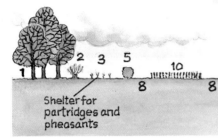
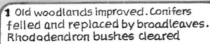

Shelter for partridges and pheasants

Grazing for sheep

Burn

Figure 12.3 'Sympathetic' farming

1 Old woodlands improved. Conifers felled and replaced by broadleaves. Rhododendron bushes cleared
2 Existing broadleaves coppiced
3 New broadleaves planted
4 Rectangular field corners rounded-off by planting broadleaves and shrubs
5 200 year old hedgerows renovated by planting hawthorn and dog-rose
6 Farm pond renovated
7 Wetlands beside burn restored
8 Broad strips of land around crops left uncultivated as a refuge for wildlife (insects, birds and mammals)
9 18 hectares of land set-aside
10 Use of chemicals on crops reduced to a minimum
11 Farm steading has become a haven for bats, owls and house-martins

Farmers and the EU

Many farmers are subsidised by the European Union (EU) because they find it difficult to make a living in the Scottish mountains and hills. All Scottish farmers can obtain extra grants and subsidies from the EU if they agree to (or want to):
1 **set-aside** crop land;
2 farm organically or use fewer chemicals;
3 farm less intensively;
4 keep fewer sheep and cattle;
5 look after abandoned farmland and woodland;
6 rear animals of local breeds in danger of extinction;
7 manage land for leisure uses;
8 plant trees, especially broadleaves;
9 build new farm buildings and roads.
Farmers in lowland areas are restricted by the EU as to how much milk, wheat, barley, and potatoes they can produce.

Lambing can be cold and difficult even on Ingleston Farm near Solway Firth

Figure 12.5 The large farm steading at Eaglescairnie Farm between the field with grain stubble in the foreground and the shelter belts beyond

Figure 12.6 Set-aside land in front of a recently harvested barley field above Blackford Glen, Edinburgh

13 Crofting: Old and New

A Crofting Landscape

The photograph in Figure 13.1 was taken at Tarskavaig on the island of Skye. Try to pick out the following features.

- The sharp peaks of the Cuillin mountains.
- The white-washed croft house.
- The level land where crops are grown.
- The different crops (oats, potatoes, grass) grown in narrow strips.
- The hummocky land where cattle and sheep are grazed, and peats can be cut.

Such features are often found in the crofting areas of the North West Highlands and Islands. A croft is a very small farm. The person who works it is called a crofter. The modern crofting landscape took shape in the nineteenth century. Before that farming methods and settlement were different.

Farming and Settlement in the 1700s

In the early 1700s the land was owned by the clan chiefs. Most people who worked the land paid rent to the chief and would fight for him in times of war. They lived in small groups of houses (see Figure 13.2). Crops were grown in strips of land, or rigs. Where the land was level, animals helped with ploughing. On steeper slopes, a footplough or 'cashcrom' was used. Rigs were shared out, and those closest to the houses got most of the

Figure 13.1   Tarskavaig, a crofting area in Skye

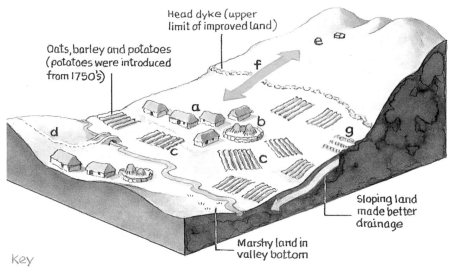

Figure 13.2   An eighteenth century Highland settlement

Key

a   Clachan: a small group of houses – stone walls and thatched roofs

b   Stackyard: haystacks surrounded by stone dyke

c   Rigs: ridges of land separated by furrows. Water drained down the furrows

d   Drove road: rough tracks along which cattle were driven to market

e   Sheiling areas: summer grazing and small stone houses

f   Transhumance: movement of animals in summer to the sheilings, returned in autumn

g   Peat banks: peat was cut for fuel

manure and peat-ash. Above the head dyke the moorland was used by everyone for summer grazing. Each year some of the small black cattle were sold. They were herded together all over the Highlands and drovers took them to Crieff and, later in the century, to Falkirk for sale at great cattle fairs or trysts. This way of life changed, especially after the Battle of Culloden (1746). Landowners found they could make more money from new breeds of sheep (Cheviot and Blackface) than from rents from people growing crops. In the worst cases during the Highland Clearances, e.g. in Strathnaver, people were driven from the land, leaving deserted villages.

Figure 13.3 Improved pasture such as this has allowed crofters to keep more animals on their land

Figure 13.4 Crofters have been given grants to have new byres built

Figure 13.5 The lime-rich machair can support many sheep and cattle, as well as being rich in wildlife

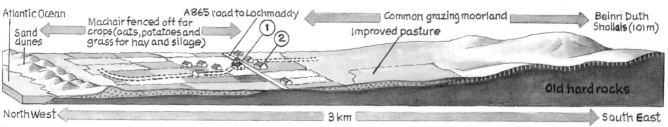

Atlantic Ocean — Sand dunes — Machair fenced off for crops (oats, potatoes and grass for hay and silage) — A865 road to Lochmaddy — ① ② — Common grazing moorland — Improved pasture — Beinn Duth Shollais (101m) — Old hard rocks

North West ← 3 km → South East

Number of crofts: 12
Number of crofters: 7 (5 part-time 2 full-time)
Average croft size: 8 ha
Animals: 500 sheep, 80 cows

Services
:::::: Township road
① Church (2 other Presbyterian churches nearby)
② General shop
A primary school is about 400m away

▓▓▓ Lime rich sand ▓▓▓ Peat
Machair: Sandy area rich with grassland and wildflowers. Supports many birds eg. dunlin, plover and corncrake. Gives rich pasture for cattle and is good for growing crops. Seaweed is added for fertiliser

Figure 13.6 Sollas, North Uist

Sollas: A Crofting Township

Figures 13.3 to 13.6 show features of crofting at Sollas, North Uist.

- Crofts are small. There is limited land to cultivate. At Sollas, the crops are grown on the machair (Figure 13.6). Seaweed is still used as a fertiliser.
- Most crofts are worked on a part-time basis. At Sollas there are two full-time crofters. They work several crofts.
- Part-time crofters have a wide range of other jobs in this area – e.g. on fish farms, as part-time postal workers, in tourism, and working at the South Uist military base.
- There are examples in the islands of 'telecrofts': computers, faxes and modems allow crofters to work for city offices.
- Crops are grown as fodder for the cattle in winter. Island crofters try to grow as much as possible, because it is expensive to ship hay from the mainland.
- While crofters have their own fields (long and narrow) for crops, they all share the moorland. This is the common grazing where they put their sheep and cattle. Some crofters have fenced off part of this land, added lime-rich sand, and sown grass. This results in a richer, improved pasture (see Figure 13.3).
- A group of crofts and their houses is called a township. Often the townships are laid out in a line along a road.

Usually there is a shop/post office, primary school, several churches, and a village hall in the township. Travelling vans regularly come from the nearest large settlement. This often includes the post-bus service, delivering mail and passengers. Because of transport costs, prices are higher in the shops here than on the mainland.
- Crofts are environmentally friendly. Crofters are given subsidies not to use weedkillers. This helps to preserve the machair wildflowers, as well as endangered birds, especially the corncrake.
- Crofting is hard work. But combined with another job, it can help to keep people in remoter areas.

14 Luffness: an Arable Farm in East Lothian

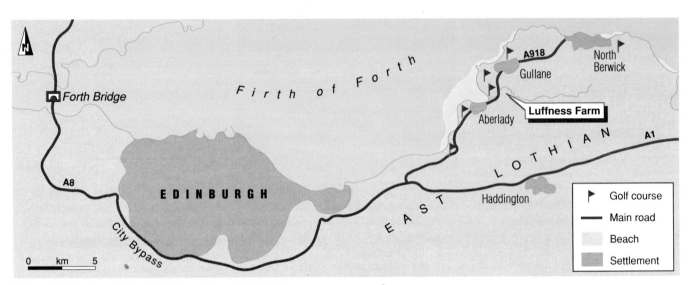

Figure 14.1   Location of Luffness Farm, East Lothian

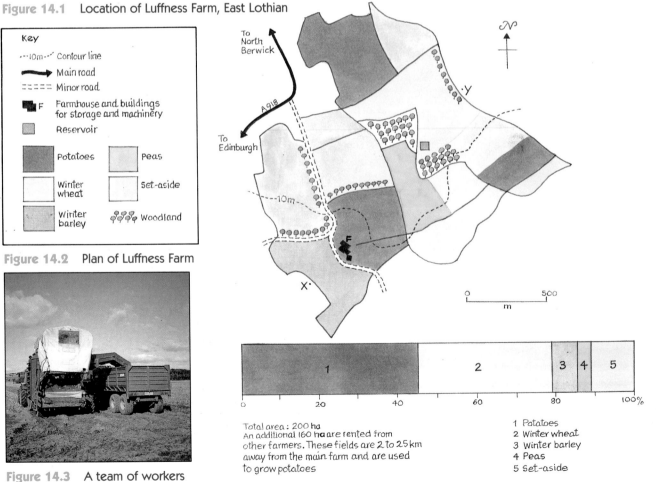

Key

- ···10m··· Contour line
- → Main road
- ===== Minor road
- F Farmhouse and buildings for storage and machinery
- Reservoir
- Potatoes
- Peas
- Winter wheat
- Set-aside
- Winter barley
- Woodland

Figure 14.2   Plan of Luffness Farm

Total area : 200 ha
An additional 160 ha are rented from other farmers. These fields are 2 to 25 km away from the main farm and are used to grow potatoes

1 Potatoes
2 Winter wheat
3 Winter barley
4 Peas
5 Set-aside

Figure 14.4   Land use at Luffness Farm

Figure 14.3   A team of workers help to sort out the potato crop

Potatoes Galore

Luffness in East Lothian (Figure 14.1) is an arable farm. This means that the farmer earns his money by growing crops. You can see the various crops on the farm plan (Figure 14.2). The land-use graph (Figure 14.4) shows that potatoes are the most important crop. This is because fields are rented from other farmers to grow more potatoes (both early and late) and two crops of potatoes are often grown in a single field. Most of the potatoes from Luffness end up on supermarket shelves. The rest are used as seed potatoes (Figure 14.5).

At harvest time the farm employs up to ten extra people to help pick, sort, clean, and pack the potatoes (Figure 14.3). There are ten full-time staff including James Armstrong, the foreman. October can be a very busy time for him, and the chart in Figure 14.8 shows a typical day's work.

Usually the potatoes are bought and sold by potato merchants. Sometimes the potatoes are packaged at Luffness and sold directly to supermarkets. Some potatoes, from the rented fields on higher land, are used for seed. They are planted the following year

Figure 14.5 Potatoes from Luffness

Luffness Farm: a Success Story

Luffness is a large and successful farm. This is partly because of the skill of the farmer and the staff. It is also because this part of East Lothian has several advantages.

- The land is level (Figure 14.6), so it is easier to use machinery on the fertile soil.
- In this part of Scotland the climate is warmer and drier.
- Even if it is too dry, the farm has its own irrigation system.
- Because it is near the sea, the farm seldom has a severe frost.

'Set-Aside' at Luffness Farm

Perhaps Luffness has been too successful. The farmer is now paid to stop growing crops on some of the land. This is known as set-aside. On arable farms like Luffness, set-aside land is left to grow grass but it cannot be grazed or cut for hay. Figure 14.2 shows the land given over to set-aside at Luffness.

Figure 14.6 This shows the level land, a large field, and North Berwick Law in the background. **Figure 14.7** (inset) In this rain shadow area, this small reservoir is needed for irrigation on Luffness Farm

Time	Typical Work
7.00 am	Start: day's work is divided between the staff.
8.30–8.45 am	Breakfast.
8.45–12.00 pm	Supervising/sharing the work, e.g. – driving one of the 6 tractors; – helping to grade potatoes.
12.00–12.30 pm	Lunch.
12.30–4.30 pm	Paperwork in the farm office. Checking with staff on potato harvester in a field rented from neighbouring farm. Reporting fault on grain drier.
4.30–7.00 pm	Break. Overtime.

Figure 14.8 James Armstrong: a day's work in October

15 Forests and the Landscape

The Great Wood of Caledon

After the end of the last Ice Age, much of Scotland slowly became covered in trees. Birch came first, followed by oak, juniper, and Scots pine. A huge wood – the Great Wood of Caledon – spread over large areas of the Highlands. Figure 15.1 shows some of the trees and wildlife which once lived there.

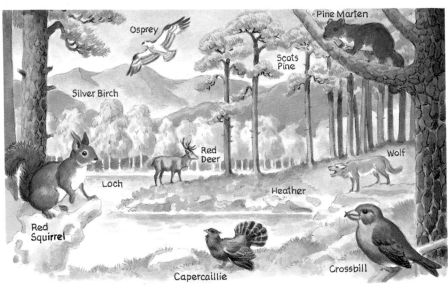

Figure 15.1   The Great Wood of Caledon

Clearing the Woodland

When the Romans came, some parts of Scotland had little woodland left. By the 1600s, only 5 per cent of the land was covered in wood. Why was it lost?

- At different times, the weather became wetter, colder, and windier. Trees died or just did not grow so well.
- Trees were felled for fuel and to build houses or ships.
- Woodland was cleared and the land was ploughed for crops.
- Room was made for sheep, cattle, and goats to graze.
- Grazing animals, especially deer, damaged young trees and prevented their growth.

Conserving the Woodland

Not all the woodland was completely cleared. Figures 15.2 and 15.3 show Bonawe,

in Argyll. Iron was made in this remote Highland village from 1753 until 1876. The iron furnace needed large supplies of charcoal as a fuel. Local trees were used, but they were carefully coppiced. Fresh shoots were harvested for the tree stumps (see inset of Figure 15.3).

Figure 15.2   Visitors beside the restored iron furnace at Bonawe, with the surviving tenements, and a large granite quarry beyond

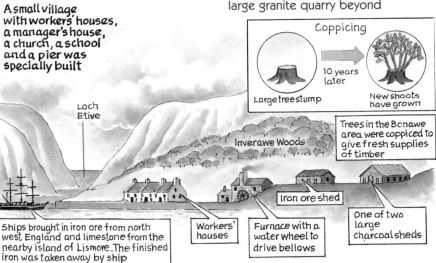

A small village with workers' houses, a manager's house, a church, a school and a pier was specially built

Coppicing

Large tree stump → 10 years later → New shoots have grown

Trees in the Bonawe area were coppiced to give fresh supplies of timber

Loch Etive

Inverawe Woods

Iron ore shed

One of two large charcoal sheds

Workers' houses

Furnace with a water wheel to drive bellows

Ships brought in iron ore from north west England and limestone from the nearby island of Lismore. The finished iron was taken away by ship

Figure 15.3   Bonawe about 1800

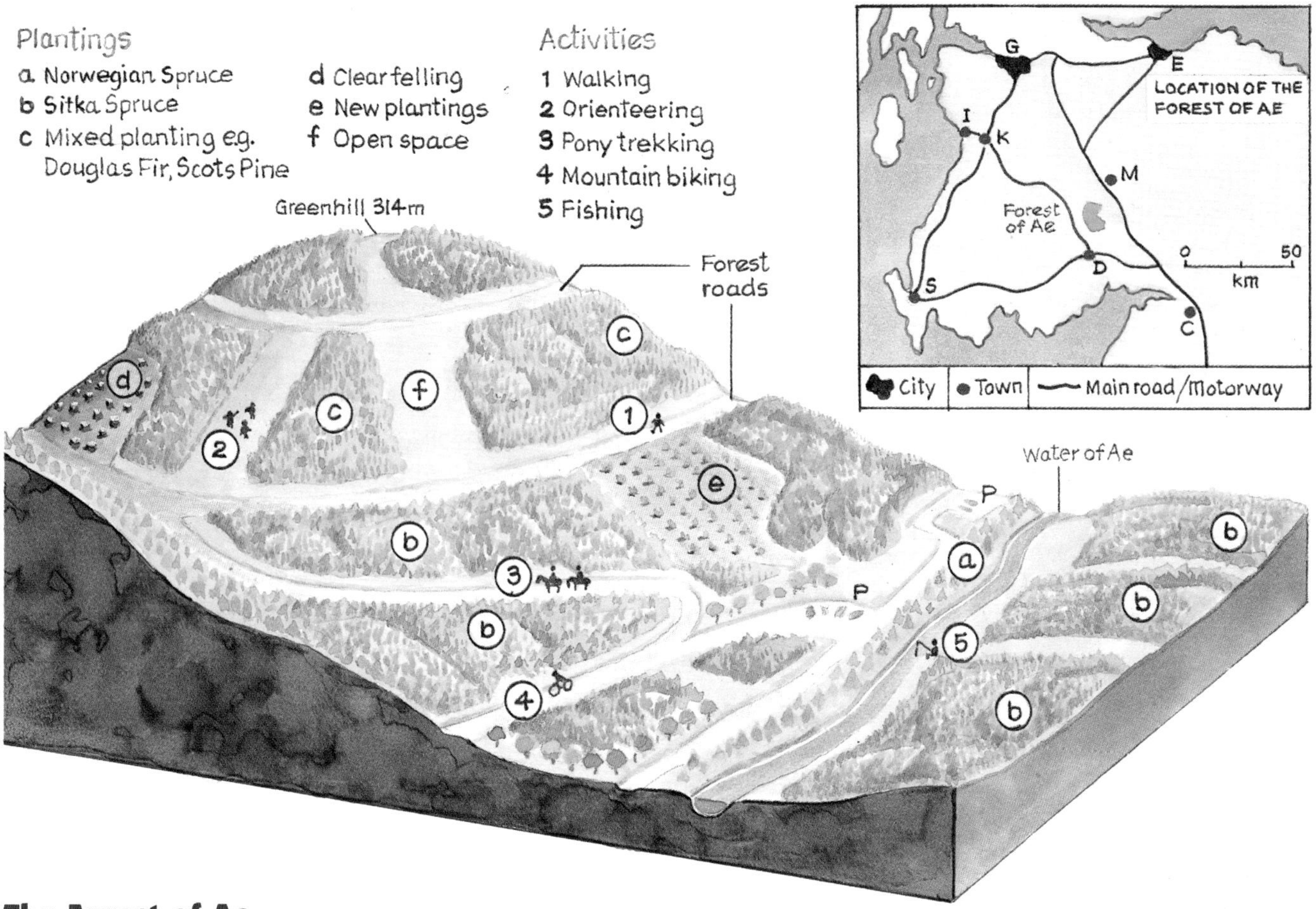

Plantings

a. Norwegian Spruce
b. Sitka Spruce
c. Mixed planting eg.
   Douglas Fir, Scots Pine
d. Clear felling
e. New plantings
f. Open space

Activities

1. Walking
2. Orienteering
3. Pony trekking
4. Mountain biking
5. Fishing

Greenhill 314m

Forest roads

Water of Ae

LOCATION OF THE FOREST OF AE

Forest of Ae

0   50
km

● City   ● Town   —— Main road/Motorway

Forests and the Landscape

Figure 15.4   Diagram of part of the Forest of Ae

The Forest of Ae

Figure 15.4 shows part of the Forest of Ae. You can locate this forest on the inset map. It is one of the many forests owned by the Forestry Commission. This was set up in 1919 after much British woodland was used up in the 1914–18 world war.

Ae Forest has been developed for over 60 years. Most of the wood goes to sawmills and is used for building. The rest goes to a pulpmill at Irvine, and to make chipboard.

A variety of trees is grown in the forest: in the early days Norway spruce was planted, but Sitka spruce is now the main species. As the older trees are felled, open spaces are created and a mixture of trees, including broadleaves, are now planted. This is to make the forest look attractive.

Forests like this have many kilometres of forest roads. Lorries use these to take away the timber when it is felled. The roads are also popular with walkers – often large groups on sponsored walks – as well as mountain bikers and pony trekkers. Orienteering clubs come from northern England and Central Scotland to the Forest of Ae. Nowadays fewer people work in the forest than 40 years ago. More machinery is used to fell the trees, although horses have recently been used to take out the timber. Forest rangers are now employed to help the public enjoy the forests and appreciate the wildlife.

Figure 15.5   The Water of Ae flows through Ae Forest

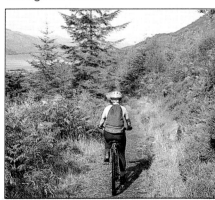

Figure 15.6   Mountain biker on trail in the Forest

16 Energy and the Landscape

Figure 16.1 In Tarskavaig, peats are cut in May, left to dry, and stacked like this

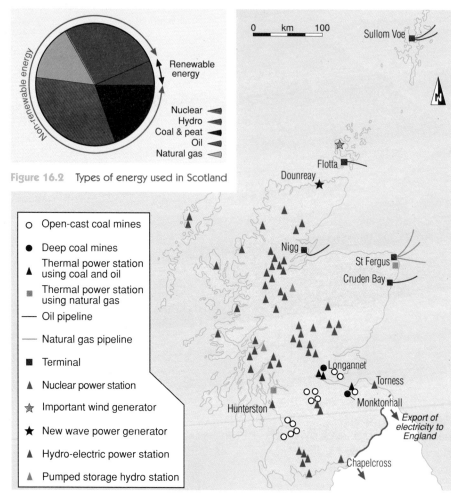

Figure 16.2 Types of energy used in Scotland

Figure 16.3 Scotland: fuel and power

Although a small country, Scotland has a rich variety of energy resources. Figure 16.2 shows that we use mainly **non-renewable** resources. Some of these are **fossil fuels** – peat, oil, natural gas and coal.

Peat (see Figure 16.1) is not produced in large amounts. It is used for fuel in many croft houses, and when making some whiskies.

Natural gas and oil, piped from the North Sea since 1975, have affected many parts of Scotland. Many jobs were created, oil is a very important export, and natural gas is important for heating and electricity. Peterhead has one of Europe's largest gas-burning power stations.

Coal has been the main fuel used in houses, factories, and railways in the past 200 years. Figure 16.4 shows some of the problems caused by coal mining. But **reclamation** is taking place. Most of Scotland's coal now comes from open-cast workings. There can be complaints about noise and dust, but once the coal is taken out the land is restored.

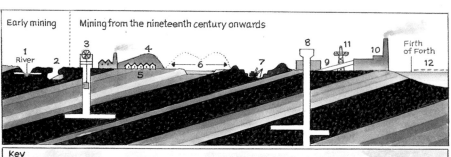

Key

1 Early mining development by monks – cut short horizontal tunnels to mine the coal and drain the water
2 Bell pit - worked by family labour
3 Steam driven winding gear and water pumps
4 Coal bing
5 Mining village - rows of terraced housing e.g. Lochgelly, Newtongrange
6 Reclaimed area - bings removed, hollows filled. Used for recreation e.g. Lochore Meadows Country Park (sailing, fishing, golf, nature reserve)

7 Opencast coal site: main source of Scottish coal
8 Modern deep coal mine - 2 working in Scotland
9 Conveyor belt
10 Coal fired thermal power station e.g. Longannet
11 Pylons - part of the National Grid system
12 Land reclaimed using coal ash

 Coal

Figure 16.4 Coal mining and the landscape

Energy and the Landscape

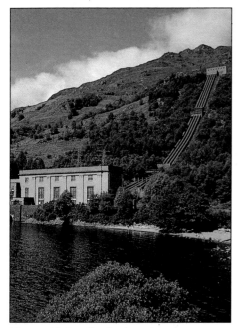

Figure 16.5 The hydro-electric power station at Sloy

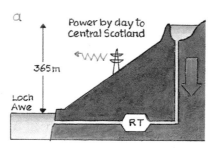

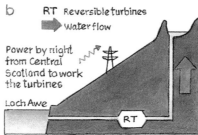

Cruachan is one of 2 pumped storage schemes. Water flows from the small high level loch to generate electricity during the day (diagram a). At night water is pumped back up into the small loch from Loch Awe

Figure 16.6 The dam built in the corrie below Ben Cruachan's summit gives a limited supply of water for the power station inside the mountain

Nuclear power stations like Torness in East Lothian (see Figure 16.7) and Hunterston in Ayrshire produce 50 per cent of Scotland's electricity. They use small amounts of uranium as fuel. When deciding where to build such a station, planners look for:

- a large area of level land;
- solid rock to take the weight of the reactor;
- a coastal green-field site near a railway.

Not everybody is happy with nuclear power. Many worry about serious risks from radiation leaks, and the disposal of waste fuel. Others claim that such stations are safe, and unlike fossil fuel power stations do not contribute to **global warming** or **acid rain**.

Hydro-electric power is the most important **renewable** energy source in Scotland. Heavy rain, steep slopes, rivers, and lochs make Scotland suitable for hydro power. Water carried through

Figure 16.7 The coastal site of Torness nuclear power station

tunnels and pipes from Loch Sloy turns the turbines in the power station (see Figure 16.5). Great engineering skills were required to build the 60 or so hydro power stations in Scotland. They have been very important in taking electricity to the remoter parts of the Highlands.

Renewable energy and conservation

Only about 6 per cent of Scotland's energy is renewable – almost entirely hydro power. Other possibilities have been experimented with or discussed, including wave and tidal power.

17 Caring for the Countryside

Conserving, or caring, for, Scotland's countryside is very important. The logo at the top of this column is that of Scottish Natural Heritage. This is the most important of the conservation agencies. The others include:

- The National Trust for Scotland;
- The Scottish Wildlife Trust;
- The Royal Society for the Protection of Birds.

The government, through the Scottish Office and the local authorities, also helps to care for the countryside.

In most countries, the wildest and most unspoilt areas are protected by being declared National Parks. Scotland has none, but there are several ways in which the countryside is protected by the government (see Figure 17.8). These may be:

1 National Scenic Areas;
2 National Nature Reserves;
3 Environmentally Sensitive Areas;
4 Sites of Special Scientific Interest (SSSIs);
5 Special Areas of Conservation;
6 Regional Parks;
7 Country Parks;
8 **Green Belts**, around the big cities.

Unfortunately, these often cause conflict, since the land is usually privately owned.

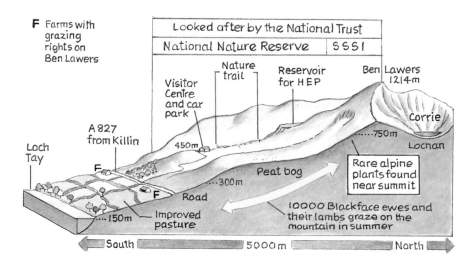

Ben Lawers is in an area of spectacular scenery. The glaciated mountains attract climbers, walkers and skiers. Other people come to look at the rare plants eg. moss campion, Alpine Lady's-Mantle, gentian.

The many visitors result in erosion of the paths above the nature trail. Centuries of grazing by livestock have resulted in the disappearance of woodland from the mountain slopes

Figure 17.1   Ben Lawers: a conservation area in Perthshire

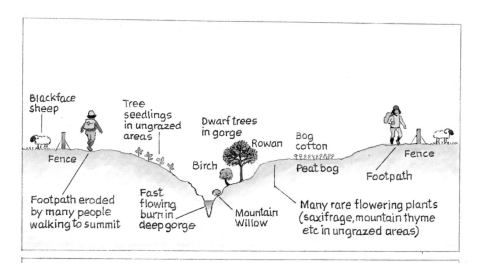

Ben Lawers is protected in three different ways. Most of the mountain is in the care of the National Trust. Part of this area is a National Nature Reserve. The

Nature Trail has been enclosed with a fence to keep out the sheep. There is an SSSI just below the summit to protect the rare flowers

Figure 17.2   Enclosed Nature Trail on Ben Lawers

There may also be disagreements with the Forestry Commission, the electricity boards, and companies wanting to quarry sands and gravels. Two good examples of conservation areas with problems are Ben Lawers and the Cairngorms (see Figures 17.1, 17.2, 17.7).

Figure 17.3 Rocks protect the dwarf willow tree and Alpine Lady's Mantle growing by the side of the burn on the Ben Lawers' Nature Trail

Figure 17.4 Repairs have had to be made to footpaths affected by erosion such as this one above the Ben Lawers' Nature Trail

Figure 17.5 Visitors caught by a summer squall of rain on the Ben Lawers' Nature Trail

Figure 17.6 a) In summer the car park beside the Ben Lawers' Visitor Centre is often full   b) A rare gentian which grows from seed every year near the summit of Ben Lawers   c) This is an area heavily grazed by Blackface sheep

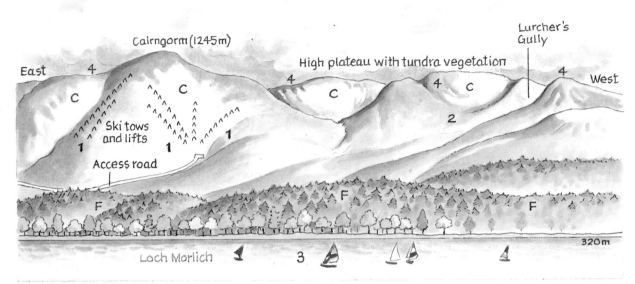

Key

C Deep snow lies for most of the year in north-facing corries

F Natural woodland eg. Scots Pine (part of the Caledonian Forest)

1 Skiing areas (less than 9 km²) where vegetation is damaged

2 Undamaged area. Developers have tried to extend skiing into Lurcher's Gully

3 Sailing and canoeing on Loch Morlich. There is a campsite and youth hostel on the northern shore

4 Areas used by walkers and climbers

Figure 17.7   Cairngorm: a National Scenic Area

Cairngorm: a National Scenic Area

The area shown in Figure 17.7 is rich in wildlife, with red deer, red squirrels, pine martens, golden eagles, peregrine falcons, ospreys, red grouse, ptarmigan, snow buntings, and dotterels. Some of the Alpine plants found on Ben Lawers are also found on the plateau. Most of the Cairngorms Plateau is a National Nature Reserve.

The Cairngorms

As at Ben Lawers, there are several ways in which the Cairngorms are protected:

- it is a National Scenic Area because of its corries, deep valleys, and high plateau;

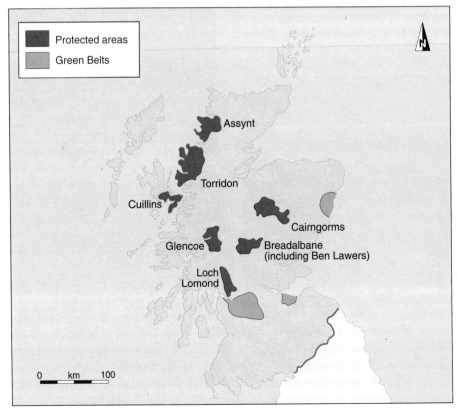

Figure 17.8   Some protected areas in Scotland

- most of it is an SSSI because of its wildlife and plantlife. Some of the original Caledonian Forest is found near Loch Morlich;
- the RSPB have bought a small area to protect rare birds, e.g. the ospreys at Loch Garten.

The area faces several problems because of the many people who want to visit it. These include:

- erosion of footpaths;
- litter on the plateau;
- erosion of the ski-runs.

Permission has been twice refused to extend skiing into Lurcher's Gully.

Figure 17.8 shows some of the main conservation areas in Scotland, including the Cairngorms.

In June 1995, the National Trust for Scotland took over the Mar Lodge Estate in the Cairngorms (Figure 17.10). This vast estate of over 314 km^2 rises from the Upper Dee Valley to the plateau summit of the Cairngorms. It is of vital importance as a true wilderness area, including remnants of the Caledonian Pine Forest. It is hoped that this natural woodland will increase naturally if the number of red deer is reduced. The estate will be conserved but visitors will be allowed free access.

There have been proposals to extend the skiing areas on the Cairngorms. These have resulted in disagreements about the proper use of the area.

Figure 17.9 Cairngorm land use conflicts

Caring for the Countryside

Figure 17.10 Looking north over Mar Lodge towards the snow-capped plateau of the Cairngorms

18 Settlements and Sites

Figure 18.1 The crannog at Loch Olabhat, Lewis, is possibly one of the oldest island dwellings in Scotland

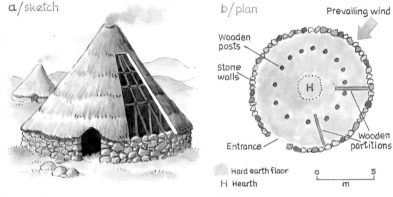

a/sketch

b/plan

Prevailing wind

Wooden posts

Stone walls

H

Entrance

Wooden partitions

Hard earth floor

H Hearth

0   5
m

Figure 18.2 A Highland house (about 3500 years ago)

We all live in a settlement of one sort or another. A settlement can vary in size from a single house to a large city with hundreds of thousands of people.

Early Settlements and Sites

The first known settlements began when the earliest settlers came to Scotland about 8500 years ago. Over many years different people arrived:

- the earliest came to hunt, fish, gather fruits and nuts;
- later, people came to farm, often building houses like those in Figures 18.1 and 18.2;
- some came as soldiers, e.g. the Romans;
- others wanted to start religious settlements, e.g. St Columba;
- at first, the Vikings came as raiders but later settled as farmers (Figure 18.3).

Whatever their reasons for settling, a suitable site had to be found. This is the land on which the settlement is built. All these settlers looked for suitable natural advantages (Figure 18.4).

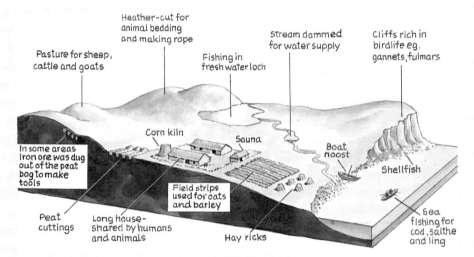

Heather-cut for animal bedding and making rope

Pasture for sheep, cattle and goats

Fishing in fresh water loch

Stream dammed for water supply

Cliffs rich in birdlife eg. gannets, fulmars

Corn kiln

Sauna

Boat noost

In some areas iron ore was dug out of the peat bog to make tools

Peat cuttings

Long house-shared by humans and animals

Field strips used for oats and barley

Hay ricks

Shellfish

Sea fishing for cod, saithe and ling

Figure 18.3 A Viking settlement in Shetland

We're looking for some of these natural advantages

Timber and/or stone for building

Protection from enemies

Level land for building

A good supply of water

A crossing or bridging point

Shelter

Maximum sunshine

A dry place

A place to pull up our ships

Fuel. wood/coal

Figure 18.4 Selecting a Site

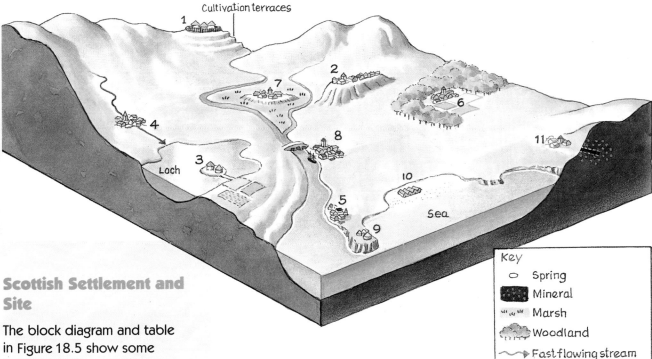

Cultivation terraces

Loch

Sea

Key
- ⬭ Spring
- ▨ Mineral
- 〰 Marsh
- ⬗ Woodland
- 〜➤ Fast flowing stream

Scottish Settlement and Site

The block diagram and table in Figure 18.5 show some Scottish settlements. You can see the natural advantages the settlers looked for. Often settlements had more than one natural advantage, and they have grown into a town or city. In some cases (e.g. Stirling) there are famous historic buildings on the original site, and these are popular with tourists (Figure 18.7). Visitors also go to abandoned sites (e.g. 1 and 3 in Figure 18.5) to see the remains of what once might have been a busy settlement. They may try to find out how the people lived and where they came from. Studying place names helps (Figure 18.6).

Number	Scottish examples	Site and why it was chosen
1	Tap o' Noth	Hilltop for defence
2	Stirling, Dumbarton	Volcanic plug – for defence
3	Loch Tay crannogs	Shallow water, opposite fertile land, defence
4	Dollar, Alva	Fast-flowing water to power mills
5	Ayr, Inverness	At the mouth of a river
6	Haddington	Fertile land in forest clearing
7	Errol	A dry point surrounded by marshland
8	Perth, Dumfries	River crossing, highest point upriver for ships
9	Burghead	Cliff top at end of promontory – defence
10	Avoch, Fraserburgh	Level coastal land
11	Wanlockhead	Near a mineral, e.g. lead

Figure 18.5 Scottish settlement and site

Figure 18.6 Scottish place names

Place name origin	Part of place name	Meaning
Gaelic	Inver_____	Mouth of a river
	Aber_____	Mouth of a river
	Dun_____	A fort or hill
	Tober_____	A well
Norse (Viking)	Kirk_____	A church
	_____vik/wick	A bay
	_____ness	A cape or headland
Anglo-Saxon	_____ham	A village

Figure 18.7 Looking west over the site of Stirling. You should be able to pick out the castle and the Old Town on the crag and tail, above the meanders of the River Forth

19 Changing Villages

Figure 19.1 Swanston Village on the edge of the Pentlands

The 'Fermtouns'

By the 1700s many people in Scotland worked on the land and lived in small groups of houses called 'fermtouns'. The houses were made of drystone walls with thatched roofs of heather, reeds, or straw. Swanston, on the outskirts of Edinburgh, gives an idea of what a fermtoun looked like. Today it is a lot tidier, and there are no cattle or middens. The owners now work in Edinburgh, but it is one of the few remaining fermtouns. Most had been changed into large, single farmsteads by the 1800s.

Other Touns

Larger touns often grew up around a church or mill (Figures 19.2 and 19.3). In the 'kirktoun' the church was often located at a crossroads. This let people from nearby fermtouns easily get to the kirk or to the weekday market. Often the 'milltoun' grew up where a fast-flowing stream left higher ground. Originally

Figure 19.2 Sketch of a Milltoun

the mill was used to grind oats and barley. By the 1700s, however, a linen mill might have been built to replace the cornmill. Locally grown flax was often used to make the linen after being soaked in a pond to soften it.

Planned Villages

At the same time as farming was changing from the seventeenth to the nineteenth centuries (page 26), new villages were built. Over 300 different villages were planned and built. There were various types.

- Some were new farming villages to replace the fermtouns. Athelstaneford in East Lothian is an example (Figure 19.4).
- New fishing villages were started, e.g. Ullapool on Loch Broom.
- Others were factory villages with new textile mills, e.g. New Lanark and Luncarty.

Figure 19.3 Sketch of a Kirktoun

Figure 19.4 Athelstaneford, a planned village, is now a dormitory settlement

Luncarty: a Changing Village

All settlements, large or small, change in different ways. Some of these changes can be seen at Luncarty, a small village 6 km north of Perth.

Changing Function

Luncarty was founded in 1752 by William Sandeman, a Perth businessman. The village grew up around a bleachworks for coarse linen cloth. The cloth was laid out on the level land and was finished off in the water-powered mill. Once, over 300 people worked at the mill. It survives today, employing 120 people (Figure 19.8), and still finishes cloth. Most villagers now travel to work in Perth, so Luncarty is a dormitory settlement and does not have many services. In fact there are fewer services than in 1945 (Figure 19.7).

Changing Population

You will see that Luncarty's population has increased since 1945. The village has grown because it is only ten minutes by car from Perth and many people like to live in the country and still be close to towns and cities for jobs and services.

Changing Shape and Land Use

If you look at the two block diagrams in Figures 19.5 and 19.8, you can see that new housing estates have been built on farmland. Villas and bungalows now stand close to what were once farm cottages. These, and the mill cottages, have been sold and modernised. Even the mill manager's house is now an old folk's home.

Figure 19.6 Modern bungalow and former mill-owner's house, now an old people's home, at Luncarty

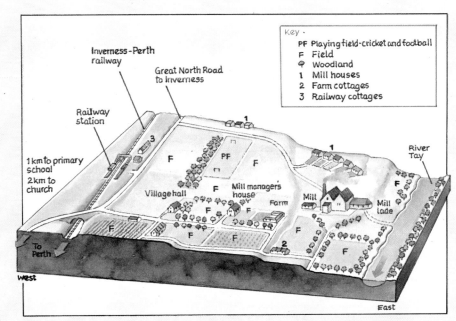

Figure 19.5 Luncarty in 1945

Year	1945	Today
Population	500	1200
Services		
Railway station	Open	Closed
Recreation club	1	2
Primary school	1	1
Church	1	Shared with neighbouring village
Shop/Post office	1	1
Shop	1	–
Garage	1	–
Blacksmith	1	–
Bus services	About 30/day (3 companies)	About 12/day (1 company)

Figure 19.7 Luncarty: changing population and services

Changing Villages

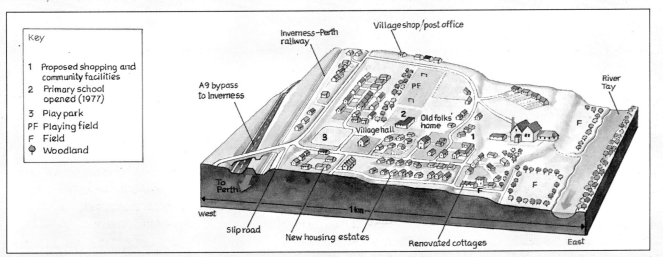

Figure 19.8 Luncarty today

20 Feshertoons: Old and New

Figure 20.1 shows a fishing village or 'feshertoon' (as it is spoken) typical of north east Scotland. In the past 100 years there have been many changes in these villages, the fishing industry, and in the waters offshore.

Feshertoons and Feshin: Nineteenth Century

The following passage is written in Doric, widely spoken in the area then and now. (See page 68.)

There's mony smaa feshertoons alaang th' Nor East coast. Fyles, toons lik Pennan an Gamrie wis biggit oot o sicht in ablo th' cliffs, atween rock and sea. Afore th'eer nineteen bunder, smaa sailin boaties caa'd yawls eesit lang lines an catchit haddock, cod, an ling. Feshin's a sair trauchle – it wid gar ye greet fyles. Aabody en th' faimly hid tae gie a haan. Faan th' men wis aa awaa at th' feshin, th' weemen, loons, an quines helpit wi shielin th' mussels an baitin th' lines. Thi guttit an driet th' fesh, syne, humphin creels on thir baacks, an selt them tae kintra fowk. Fowk en th' feshertoons wis aye gey close til een anither an mony wis richt gweed-livin.

Feshertoons and Fishing Today

Today many of the feshertoons are dormitory villages. New

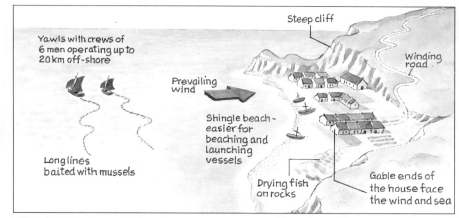

Figure 20.1 A nineteenth century 'Feshertoon'

Figure 20.2 This gives a good idea of a purse seine boat and of the size of its net

Figure 20.3 This fish processing plant provides many much needed jobs

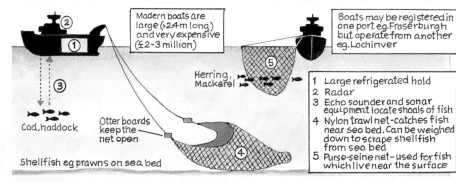

Figure 20.4 Modern fishing methods

housing has been built above the original toon. Fishing mainly now takes place from feshertoons that grew into small towns, especially Peterhead and Fraserburgh. This was because:

- they built harbours which could handle many boats. This was very important

with the boom in herring fishing from the 1850s
- railway lines were built to these towns. Herring had to be gutted, packed into barrels and crates, and sent for sale as soon as possible

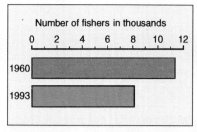

Figure 20.5 Fishers employed at Scottish ports

Number of fishers in thousands

1960

1993

Use larger net meshes and let young fish escape

Make fishermen tie up their boats and not go to sea for so many days

Limit the amount of each type of fish to be caught

FOR SALE

Fishermen are paid to sell their boats and give up catching fish

Figure 20.6 The EU and overfishing: some counter-measures

Less fish caught

⇩

Fewer fishers/boats at sea

⇩

Fewer jobs on shore, e.g.
• processing fish
• building/repairing boats
• transporting fish

⇩

More unemployed people

⇩

Young people migrate

Figure 20.7 Unemployment in a fishing settlement

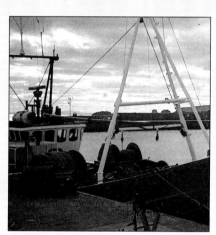

Figure 20.8 St Monance – this fishing harbour in the East Neuk of Fife is not as busy as it used to be. Declining catches and EU regulations affect the local economy

Fewer Fish and Fewer Fishers

Although a port such as Peterhead is one of the largest in Europe for cod and haddock, the Scottish fishing industry is declining. The graph in Figure 20.5 shows that there are fewer fishers than in 1960. There are also fewer fish because of overfishing. Overfishing is the result of:

- improved technology, e.g. echo-sounders, making it much easier to find the fish;
- modern boats which are very expensive to buy, equip, and run. Skippers need good catches to pay for all of this;
- too many boats chasing fewer fish. These boats are not just from Scotland, but from other EU countries such as Denmark and France.

To try to stop overfishing, the EU has a Common Fisheries Policy (Figure 20.6). If overfishing is not stopped, many people (and not just those who go to sea) will be out of work.

Pollution is another problem: fish and seals and birds are dying because of it. The problem is particularly serious in the North Sea.

About half of the pollution in the North Sea comes from the rivers flowing into it.

Excuse me speaking with my beak full of sand eels but I want to complain about all that you human beings are doing to the North Sea

1 Over 300 oil and gas platforms – problem of leaks
2 North Sea is one of the world's busiest – over 400 000 sailings and 150 accidents a year – problem of oil pollution
3 Millions of tonnes of sand and gravel are dredged from sea bed – disturbs fish spawn and sand eels
4 Sewage from some towns and cities
5 Industrial pollution from factories, power stations and oil refineries
6 Pollution from farms e.g. from fertilisers and pesticides
7 Industrial fishing – sand eels are dredged from the sea bed and made into fish-meal. This kills off an important source of food for sea birds

About half of the pollution in the North Sea comes from the rivers flowing into it

Figure 20.9 Pollution in the North Sea

21 The Changing Highlands and Islands

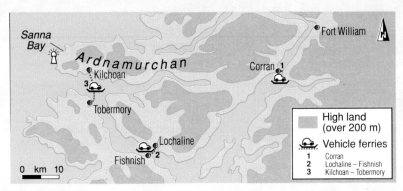

Figure 21.1   Location of Ardnamurchan

Figure 21.2   The ferry, operating in summer between Kilchoan and Oban, is popular with tourists

Ardnamurchan

Ardnamurchan lighthouse is the most westerly point on the Scottish mainland. A journey there usually means taking the Corran ferry and then a two-hour drive along a mainly single-track road. This twists and turns along the coast towards the village of Kilchoan (population 150 in 1991).

New People

Figure 21.4 shows that after many years of falling population, numbers are slowly increasing.

- Some people have retired there. Although isolated, it has attractive scenery and a quiet way of life.
- Some people, often with children, have found jobs, sometimes by starting own businesses.

New Jobs

Some of the people in Kilchoan are crofters (see page 29), but crofting is only a part-time job. Among new jobs in the area are:

- fish-farming, encouraged by the Highlands and Islands Enterprise;

- tourism. This is helped by the rugged, volcanic scenery; the sandy beaches, e.g. at Sanna; the rich wildlife; and the various trips by ferry to Mull (Figure 21.2). Kilchoan's population increases in summer as holiday homes are let (Figure 21.3).

New Pupils

New people and new jobs mean that the children at Kilchoan Primary School include those born locally and 'incomers'. In the school, all the children learn together about the local area and its Gaelic heritage.

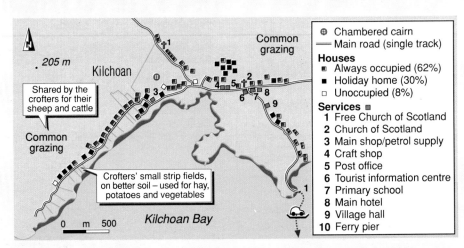

Figure 21.3   Kilchoan

Chambered cairn
Main road (single track)
Houses
- Always occupied (62%)
- Holiday home (30%)
- Unoccupied (8%)
Services
1 Free Church of Scotland
2 Church of Scotland
3 Main shop/petrol supply
4 Craft shop
5 Post office
6 Tourist information centre
7 Primary school
8 Main hotel
9 Village hall
10 Ferry pier

Shared by the crofters for their sheep and cattle

Crofters' small strip fields, on better soil – used for hay, potatoes and vegetables

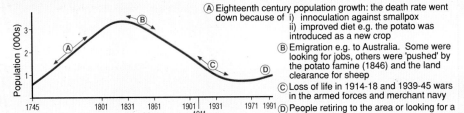

Figure 21.4   Population change in Ardnamurchan

(A) Eighteenth century population growth: the death rate went down because of i) inoculation against smallpox ii) improved diet e.g. the potato was introduced as a new crop

(B) Emigration e.g. to Australia. Some were looking for jobs, others were 'pushed' by the potato famine (1846) and the land clearance for sheep

(C) Loss of life in 1914-18 and 1939-45 wars in the armed forces and merchant navy

(D) People retiring to the area or looking for a new way of life

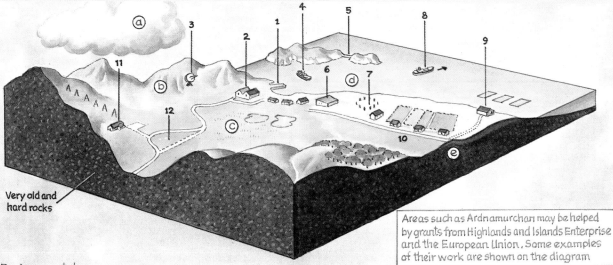

Very old and
hard rocks

Areas such as Ardnamurchan may be helped
by grants from Highlands and Islands Enterprise
and the European Union. Some examples
of their work are shown on the diagram

**Environmental
difficulties**

ⓐ Heavy rainfall from 1500mm to
over 3500mm in the Ben Nevis area

ⓑ Steep slopes with poor thin soil

ⓒ Gentle slopes and heavy rainfall
encourage acid peat soils

ⓓ Isolation of the sea lochs and the
islands means higher transport
costs and dearer goods in the shops

ⓔ Limited areas of fertile land

1 New pier for fishing boats at Lochinver

2 New advance factories and workshops

3 Co-operation with BT to improve
telecommunications

4 Improving ferry facilities eg.Yell-Unst-Fetlar

5 Building a new causeway from Barra to Vatersay

6 New swimming pool and leisure
facilities eg.Mallaig

7 New visitor centres eg. Callanish Heritage
Centre on Lewis

8 Fishing for less familiar types of fish e.g.scabbard

9 Fish farming and experimenting with new
species eg.halibut

10 Help was given to the Assynt crofters to buy
the North Lochinver estate

11 Building of restaurant at the Glencoe Ski centre

12 Road improvement schemes eg.Western Isles

Figure 21.5   Helping the Western Highlands and Islands: a difficult
environment

Highland areas, including Ardnamurchan, have
changed greatly in the last 30 years. Despite
the problems (see Figure 21.5), the overall
population has increased. While there
are still areas of high unemployment,
e.g. the Western Isles, new jobs have
been created. Many are as a result of
North Sea oil, help from the
European Union and Highlands
and Islands Enterprise

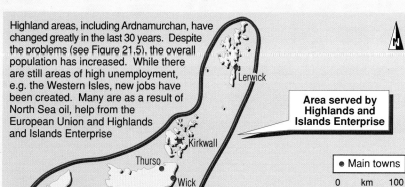

Area served by
**Highlands and
Islands Enterprise**

• Main towns

0   km   100

Figure 21.6   Highland and Island
Development

Figure 21.7   Callanish Ltd, on the island of
Lewis, was set up in 1986. It now employs
32 people, producing high-value medical
products. These are based on fish and
vegetable oils

Figure 21.8   Improved
telecommunications have helped
reduce isolation in the Scottish
Highlands

Figure 21.9   Modern technology
allows people to carry out office
work from their homes in remote
areas

22 Resorts and Market Towns

- Edinburgh – a capital city.
- Ullapool – a fishing port.
- St Andrews – a holiday resort.

The above list tells us something about a settlement's function. That describes what a settlement does.

Figure 22.1 The Promenade at Largs

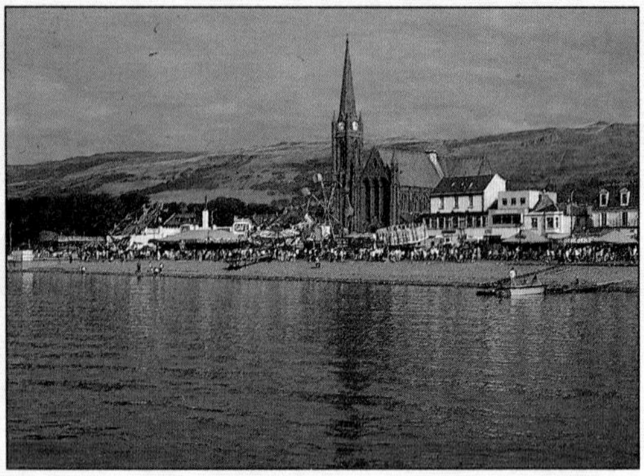

Figure 22.2 The setting of Largs on the Firth of Clyde

Largs – A Holiday Resort

Figure 22.2 shows the sea front at Largs – one of the famous seaside resorts on the Firth of Clyde. This was a small fishing port in the eighteenth century. It grew into a resort because:

- sea bathing was believed to be healthy;
- by the 1890s most people had at least a week's holiday (usually without pay);
- resorts like Largs were more accessible. Many Glaswegians came 'doon the watter' by steamer or by railway, especially during the Glasgow Fair fortnight.

By the 1930s, Larg's population increased by 25 000 each summer. The better off stayed in a hotel or boarding house. Many rented rooms in people's houses. With its fresh air, promenade, Italian cafés, cinemas and shows, Largs offered a welcome break from the crowded smoky city and from the factory and shipyard hooter.

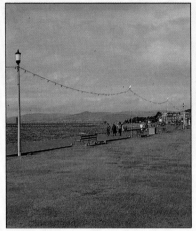

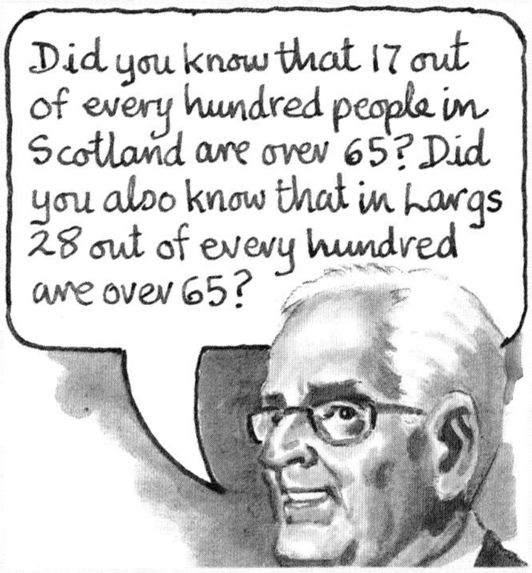
Did you know that 17 out of every hundred people in Scotland are over 65? Did you also know that in Largs 28 out of every hundred are over 65?

Figure 22.3 It's a matter of fact

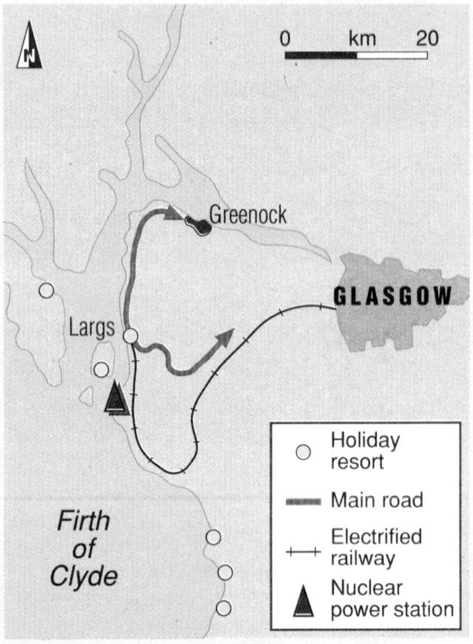
0
km
20
Greenock
GLASGOW
Largs
Firth of Clyde
Holiday resort
Main road
Electrified railway
Nuclear power station

Figure 22.4 Location of Largs: travelling to work

Changing Functions

Largs and other resorts are no longer so popular with Scottish holiday makers. Today a flight to the Mediterranean for a fortnight is often cheaper. How has Largs changed?

- The town is now popular for day trips and short breaks. Most people travel by car, and you can see the promenade in Figure 22.1.
- It is a dormitory settlement. People like to live here and travel to work in Glasgow, or the IBM factory at Greenock, or Hunterston Nuclear Power Station (Figure 22.4).
- Like other resorts, Largs is popular with retired people. Over the past 15 years, 14 hotels have either been changed to nursing homes or demolished to build flats for the elderly (Figure 22.3).

Figure 22.5 A livestock auction at Perth's Agricultural Centre

Perth – A Market Town

Figure 22.5 shows the inside of the Perth Agricultural Centre. Perth, like the towns in the list (Figure 22.6), is a long-established market town. Market towns developed when most people worked on the land. Some of the best conditions for the growth of a market town are listed in the block diagram (Figure 22.6). In the past, there were many more towns and villages with weekly or monthly markets. It was a busy day: selling grain, horses, sheep and cattle, and hiring farm labourers. Often the market was held in the main street or market square. There are fewer market towns today. The main ones are those with good communications. During Perth's history as a market town, various market sites have been used. Three of these are shown in Figures 22.7 and 22.8.

Figure 22.8 The Agricultural Centre is located close to the western bypass

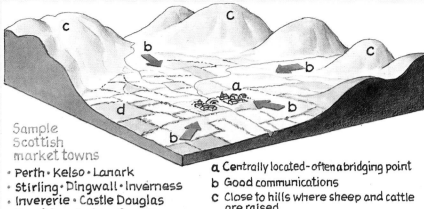

Sample Scottish market towns
- Perth • Kelso • Lanark
- Stirling • Dingwall • Inverness
- Invererie • Castle Douglas
- Dumfries • Lairg • Cupar
- Grantown on Spey

a Centrally located – often a bridging point
b Good communications
c Close to hills where sheep and cattle are raised
d Beside fertile farmland where crops are grown and livestock fattened

Figure 22.6 Setting for a market town

Figure 22.7 Perth market on the move

① A thirteenth century market

One early market was beside St John's Kirk. Animals were driven to market to be sold or slaughtered in the nearby Skinnergate

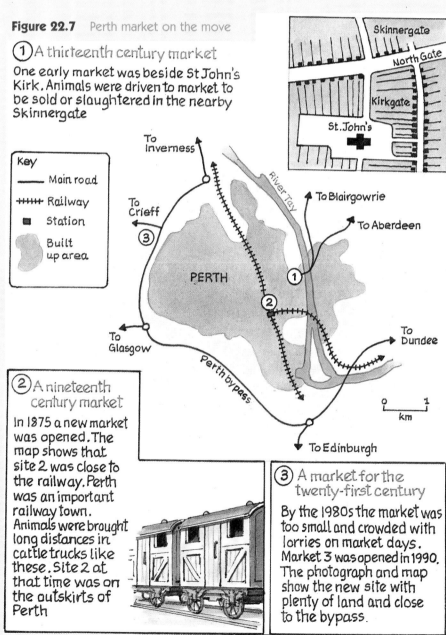

Key
— Main road
+++++ Railway
■ Station
Built up area

② A nineteenth century market

In 1875 a new market was opened. The map shows that site 2 was close to the railway. Perth was an important railway town. Animals were brought long distances in cattle trucks like these. Site 2 at that time was on the outskirts of Perth

③ A market for the twenty-first century

By the 1980s the market was too small and crowded with lorries on market days. Market 3 was opened in 1990. The photograph and map show the new site with plenty of land and close to the bypass.

23 Industrial Towns

Coatbridge

Summerhill Heritage Centre, in Coatbridge, calls itself 'Scotland's noisiest museum'. It is one of several important industrial museums. As Figure 23.1 shows, it provides evidence of coal mining; iron-working; three kinds of transport; and miners' houses.

It lies just north of the town centre of Coatbridge, an industrial town on the eastern edge of Glasgow (see Figure 23.2). Coatbridge grew rapidly from several small villages in the nineteenth century. This was because the villages were sitting on top of valuable resources such as coal; ironstone; limestone; sandstone; sands and clays.

Figure 23.3 suggests how industries in the town grew. Miners' rows and tenements were built to house the workers and their families. The Monklands Canal, and later the many railways, were built to carry the raw materials and the finished products. Heavy industries polluted the air and the rivers. Waste materials or 'slag' from the coal mines and the blast furnaces were dumped beside houses.

Coatbridge today is very different (see Figure 23.4). It is still an industrial town, but the coal mines and the iron furnaces have been closed for a long time. The oldest tenements and the miners' rows have been replaced by newer housing. There are still some engineering works, but most of the industry is now located on industrial estates.

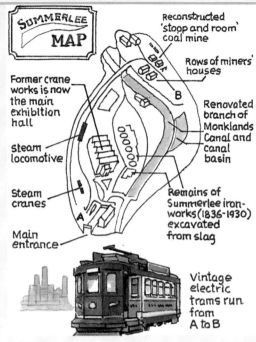

Figure 23.1   Summerlee map

Figure 23.2   Position of Coatbridge and Paisley

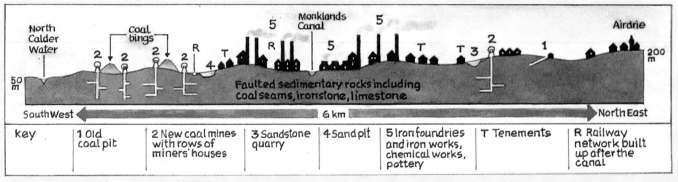

Figure 23.3   Coatbridge: the growth of industry in the nineteenth century

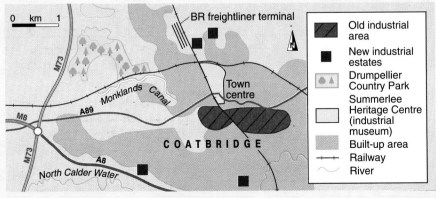

Figure 23.4   Coatbridge today

Paisley

On the western edge of Glasgow is a larger industrial town, Paisley (Figure 23.2). Paisley has twice as many people as Coatbridge. It grew up on the same kind of rolling landscape as Coatbridge, with the same rocks underneath (Figure 23.5). But its development was very different from Coatbridge.

- There was a town here several centuries before Coatbridge.
- The town grew because of the importance of the Abbey.
- It grew where important routes crossed the White Cart Water, at a place which small ships could reach from the River Clyde.
- Weaving and shoe-making were early industries.
- Coal mining was never of great importance.
- The textile industry first used local materials, wool and flax; it later used imported silk and cotton.
- Making Paisley shawls and cotton thread made the town world-famous in the nineteenth and early twentieth centuries.

Key

1 Town House
2 Tron
3 Sandhaven
4 Mercat Cross
5 The Palace
6 The Study

Industries and trade

7 Coal mined 35m under sea (1575-1625)
8 Salt pans (as many as 50 in the seventeenth century)
9 Ironsmiths (hammer**men**) made iron girdles for baking. They were sold all over Scotland
10 Exports of girdles, salt and coal to Europe

Figure 23.5 Paisley: reasons for growth

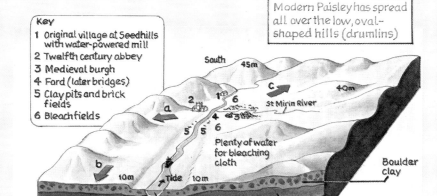

Modern Paisley has spread all over the low, oval-shaped hills (drumlins)

Key

1 Original village at Seedhills with water-powered mill
2 Twelfth century abbey
3 Medieval burgh
4 Ford (later bridges)
5 Clay pits and brick fields
6 Bleachfields

South

45m
40m

St Mirin River

Plenty of water for bleaching cloth

Boulder clay

10m   Tide   10m

North

White Cart Water flows north to join the Black Cart Water near Renfrew

Sedimentary rocks, including sandstone, limestone and coal

Routes

a To Glasgow (11km)
b To Renfrew (6km)
c To Ayr and Whithorn

Paisley grew rapidly from 1750 to 1900 both in area and population. This was because of the textile industry expanding and changing. Linen cloth was made first, then silk, and finally cotton

Thread making is still carried on in Paisley today, but far fewer people are employed. Industry has become less important to the town in the last 30 years. A major blow was the closure of the short-lived Hillman car factory, at Linwood, on the western edge of the town.

Culross

This is a very small town of a few hundred people, 14 km west of the Forth Bridge, in Fife. It grew up on the slope and shore below an abbey (Figure 23.6). It was the most important industrial centre in Scotland in the seventeenth century, more so than Paisley in this period, at a time when Coatbridge did not exist. It had a royal charter to trade with Europe. It mined coal, extracted salt from sea water, and made wrought-iron girdles for baking.

These industries have long since gone. Apart from the few shops and two schools, there is no work in the town. Culross is important today because the National Trust for Scotland has carefully restored many old buildings to show how houses were built 400 years ago. The exteriors of these houses have been conserved, but the interiors are modern except in special buildings, e.g. the Palace and the Study.

Church

Abbey House

40m

Walled garden

Ruins of sixth century monastery and thirteenth century abbey

Tanhouse Brae (very steep slope)

25m

Very steep slope

10m

High water mark

Harbour

Present shoreline

Area now reclaimed from the sea

Firth of Forth

Figure 23.6 Culross about 1750, inset photo: Culross today – notice the red pantiles and the crow-stop gables on the buildings

Industrial Towns

24 Living in Cities: Glasgow

Three out of every ten Scots live in the four main cities of Glasgow, Edinburgh, Aberdeen and Dundee. The origins of these cities are as different as the reasons for their importance today. Two have shown a recent decline in population: Glasgow and Dundee. Glasgow has lost many people, but is still Scotland's largest city, with 624 000 people.

Figure 24.1 The reconstructed Mercat Cross and Tron in front of renovated tenements in Glasgow's High Street

Figure 24.2 Tower blocks built on the sides of a drumlin in Drumchapel

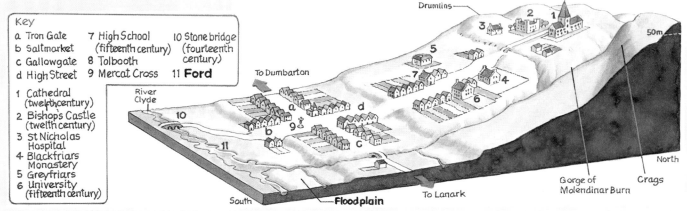

Key

a Tron Gate
b Saltmarket
c Gallowgate
d High Street

7 High School (fifteenth century)
8 Tolbooth
9 Mercat Cross

10 Stone bridge (fourteenth century)
11 **Ford**

1 Cathedral (twelfth century)
2 Bishop's Castle (twelfth century)
3 St Nicholas Hospital
4 Blackfriars Monastery
5 Greyfriars
6 University (fifteenth century)

Figure 24.3 Early Glasgow

Figure 24.3 shows where and when Glasgow began.

- The cathedral and later the university were the early reasons for its importance. The Old Town stretched southwards from Glasgow Cathedral to the River Clyde.
- Ships could not sail up the Clyde in the early days, because it was so shallow. But this was not important, since Glasgow did not face Europe.
- In the eighteenth century, the Clyde became important for Glasgow's trade with the colonies in North America.

- This led to the growth of Glasgow as a port. The river was widened, deepened, and straightened. The New Town was built westwards from the Old Town.
- Tenements, shipyards, and factories were built as the town's population and industry expanded in the nineteenth century – (1) along the Clyde eastwards and westwards; (2) southwards across the Clyde; and (3) northwards to the Monklands Canal.
- In the second half of the twentieth century, Glasgow greatly increased in area as new housing

estates were built up to 10 km from the Old Town.

Glasgow's Transport System

Glasgow has changed greatly. Factories and shipyards have closed. New industrial estates and houses have been built. Transport has been a major problem. Although Glasgow's population has dropped, traffic has increased. More people have cars, and they travel long distances to work, to shop, and for recreation. They travel to Glasgow from all the surrounding towns (see Figure 24.4), as well as from outlying areas such as Easterhouse.

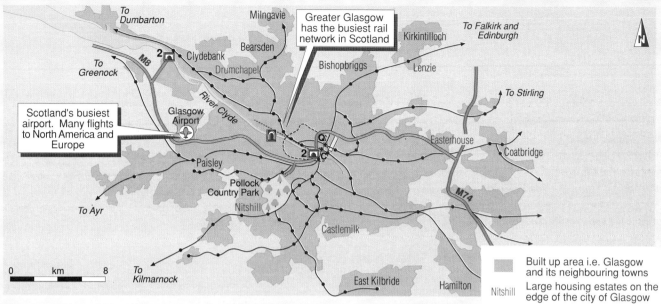

Figure 24.4 People moving in and around Greater Glasgow

Map labels:
To Dumbarton, Milngavie, Greater Glasgow has the busiest rail network in Scotland, Kirkintilloch, To Falkirk and Edinburgh, Bearsden, Clydebank, Bishopbriggs, Lenzie, M8, Drumchapel, To Greenock, River Clyde, To Stirling, Scotland's busiest airport. Many flights to North America and Europe, Glasgow Airport, Easterhouse, Coatbridge, Paisley, Q, C, Pollock Country Park, Nitshill, M74, To Ayr, Castlemilk, To Kilmarnock, East Kilbride, Hamilton

0 km 8

Legend:
- Built up area i.e. Glasgow and its neighbouring towns
- Nitshill — Large housing estates on the edge of the city of Glasgow
- Early Glasgow
- Country park
- Airport
- Railway with station
- Q Glasgow Queen Street station
- C Glasgow Central station
- Underground railway
- Motorway
- Clydeside Expressway
- Clyde Tunnel
- 1 Kingston Bridge
- 2 Erskine Bridge

Figure 24.5 Many buildings in the centre of Glasgow had to be demolished to make way for the M8 as it was built through the city centre

Figure 24.6 Several streets in the CBD such as Buchanan Street have been pedestrianised

Transport in Glasgow

Problem	Solution
Traffic jams	Building the M8 motorway through the city centre, and the M80, M77, and Clydeside Expressway
The barrier created by the River Clyde	Building the Clyde Tunnel and the Erskine Bridge
Too many people in slow-moving cars and buses in the Central Business District (CBD)	Upgrade the underground railway system which encircles the CBD
Roads choked with traffic	Provide a frequent rail service from outlying areas, e.g. Drumchapel, and from nearby towns, e.g. Paisley and Coatbridge, to the CBD

Figure 24.7 On a small scale, Glasgow's Underground provides a fast route around the CBD

Living in Cities: Glasgow

25 Living in Cities: Aberdeen

Key

1 St Machais Cathedral
  (fourteenth century)
2 King's College (University)
  (sixteenth century)
3 Spital-Gallowgate
4 Marischal College
  (University)
  (sixteenth century)
5 Castlegait, Town House,
  Tolbooth and Mercat Cross
6 Harbour and fishing village
  (Futty, later known as Footdee)
7 Export of salmon, wool, cloth
  and hides to Baltic ports
  and Campvere (Rhine Delta)

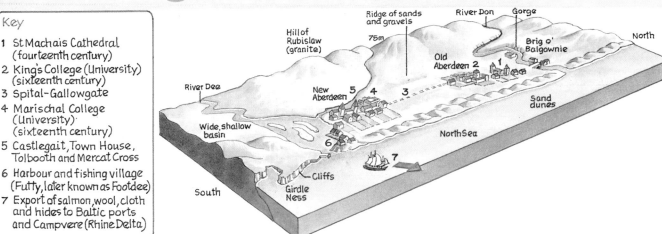

Figure 25.1 Early Aberdeen

The city of Aberdeen was two separate towns until 1891, i.e. Old and New Aberdeen. Figure 25.1 shows the sites of the two towns, at the mouths of the Rivers Don and Dee. Both towns were built at opposite ends of a low ridge of sand and gravel. Both once had castles, and universities which were united in the nineteenth century. Old Aberdeen was also important for its cathedral, while New Aberdeen became wealthy from its trade with the European ports of the North Sea and the Baltic. Figure 25.6 shows how the city has now grown west onto higher ground, as well as across to the farther banks of its two rivers. The deep valley of the River Don became important for paper and woollen mills. However, the two most important events in growth were the introduction of trawling in 1882 and the discovery of oil and gas in the North Sea from 1969 onwards. Aberdeen became the most important fishing harbour in

Scotland. Torry, a new fishing suburb, was built on the south side of the Dee estuary, as well as a new fishing boat quay, Albert Quay. In the mid-twentieth century, Aberdeen had more trawlers, more fishers, and caught and processed more fish than any other port in Scotland. Now it has lost that position to Peterhead.

Figure 25.2 Oil supply vessels make Aberdeen Harbour very busy

Work in the oil industry became very important in Aberdeen and in Grampian as a whole (see Figures 25.3 and 25.4). Aberdeen grew in size, population, and prosperity.

	1982	1992
Boatbuilding	1175	50
Textiles	1920	1250
Oil industry	32 700	47 820

Figure 25.3 Changing employment

The oil industry based in the city of Aberdeen is a major source of jobs. Many people from other parts of Scotland and from other countries were attracted to the city.

In 1982, the oil industry employed **one** out of every **four** workers in Aberdeen.

In 1992, the oil industry employed **one** out of every **three** workers in Aberdeen.

In 1992, for every **two** workers, involved in the extraction of oil from the North Sea, there were **three** workers ashore in Aberdeen.

Figure 25.4 Jobs in the oil industry

The oil industry has had three main effects on people:
1 it brought many jobs to the city;
2 unemployment is much lower than elsewhere in Scotland;
3 male workers are among the best paid in the United Kingdom.

Figure 25.5 Aberdeen's population (in thousands)

1981	1991	1993
212	215	218

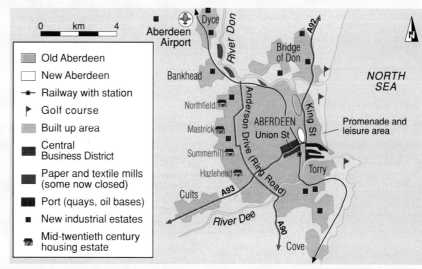

Figure 25.6 Aberdeen today

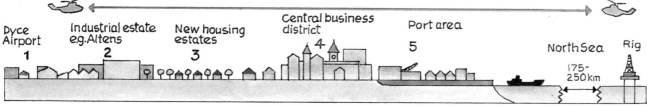

1 Dyce has become a very busy airport. Helicopter traffic to/from the rigs >50% total traffic
2 Offices, warehouses, laboratories, small factories built on new estates round the city
3 House prices have risen sharply. More than 25000 houses built in the last 20 years
4 New offices and shopping centre (St Nicholas) constructed. Hotels and restaurants have flourished
5 Port renovated. Lock gates removed. Oil support bases established

Figure 25.7 Impact of oil on Aberdeen since 1971

Aberdeen's Changing Townscape

The oil and gas rigs are a long way out in the North Sea, halfway to Norway and Denmark. The oil is brought ashore at Cruden Bay, and the gas at Peterhead, both north of Aberdeen. Yet the industry has had a major effect on the city (see Figure 25.7).

- Major oil companies, e.g. Esso, Shell, BP, and Texaco set up headquarters in vast new buildings.
- These were located on new industrial estates on the outskirts, e.g. at Dyce and Altens.
- Outlying towns and villages, e.g. Dyce, Bridge of Don, and Cove grew greatly in area. Large new housing estates were built.
- The lock gates on Victoria Dock were removed to make the whole harbour tidal. The channel was deepened to take the large oil-supply vessels. Oil field service bases were established on the quays.
- The helicopters needed to transfer crews to and from the rigs were based at Dyce. It became the busiest helicopter base in the UK.
- Aberdeen became an international centre for investment and research in the off-shore oil industry.

Figure 25.8 Like many buildings in the city, Marischal College is made of local granite

26 Living in Cities: Edinburgh

Early Edinburgh

Edinburgh was in some respects like Aberdeen in the past. Here too there were two towns, the royal burgh of Edinburgh and the church burgh of Canongate. The first grew down the 'tail' of the crag and tail from the Castle (see Figure 26.1). The second grew up the lower part of the 'tail' from Holyrood Abbey and the royal palace.

The site was however very restricted. Very tall tenements had to be built. The walled town became overcrowded and unhealthy. The planned New Town was built to the north of the Old Town in the eighteenth century. The city has grown greatly since then, taking in the port of Leith, many old villages, e.g. Dean and Corstorphine, and some small towns, e.g. South Queensferry. It has grown:

- round other hills of igneous rock, e.g. the Braid Hills;
- over the drained beds of former lochs, e.g. Corstorphine;
- on the flatter land along the shores of the Firth of Forth.

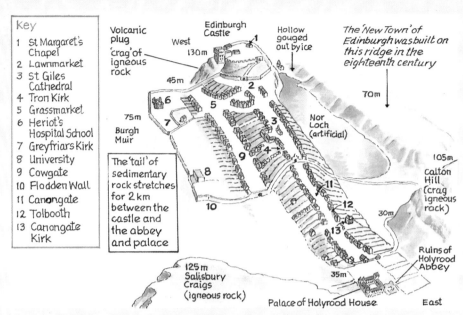

Key

1. St Margaret's Chapel
2. Lawnmarket
3. St Giles Cathedral
4. Tron Kirk
5. Grassmarket
6. Heriot's Hospital School
7. Greyfriars Kirk
8. University
9. Cowgate
10. Flodden Wall
11. Canongate
12. Tolbooth
13. Canongate Kirk

The 'tail' of sedimentary rock stretches for 2 km between the castle and the abbey and palace

The 'New Town' of Edinburgh was built on this ridge in the eighteenth century

Figure 26.1 Early Edinburgh – around 1690

Within the city, and around the built-up area, there is still a green belt, i.e. farmland and open space for recreation.

Edinburgh's CBD

The Central Business District (CBD) of Edinburgh is located partly in the Old Town but mainly in the New Town. The large offices (insurance, finance, and government) and the bank headquarters are here. There are department stores, the largest hotels, art galleries, and most of the restaurants. Fortunately, there are no tower blocks, and no urban motorway.

Edinburgh Castle and the shops in Princes Street attract many tourists, as well as local people. In addition to the department stores (e.g. Jenners, Frasers), and the multiples (e.g. Marks & Spencer, BHS, Boots, C&A, etc), there are many shops selling clothes, shoes, leisurewear and souvenirs.

Figure 26.2 Traffic, tourists and souvenir shops are notable features in the narrow Royal Mile

Figure 26.3 Major stores occupy prime sites in Prince Street, but parking and delivery are serious problems

Figure 26.4 M & S have opened another store in this new suburban shopping centre with adequate parking

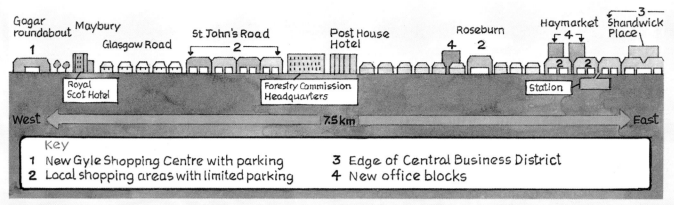

Figure 26.5 Transect from the Central Business District to the Gyle along the A8

Key
1 New Gyle Shopping Centre with parking
2 Local shopping areas with limited parking
3 Edge of Central Business District
4 New office blocks

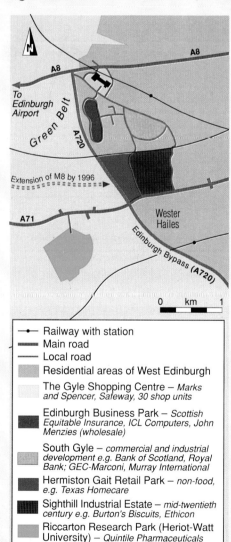

Figure 26.6 Recent developments in West Edinburgh

Reasons for Developments
1 Easy access by road (city bypass and M8).
2 Space for parking.
3 Proximity to Edinburgh Airport.

Working in Edinburgh

Of every 100 workers in Edinburgh:
- Only 14 work in factories;
- but 79 work in offices, banks, shops, hotels, restaurants, hospitals, schools, and transport, i.e. the service sector.

Many of the workers in the service sector are therefore based in the CBD. This is changing with development of suburban centres such as the Gyle and Kinnaird Park. These have eased traffic and parking in the CBD. But they could also result in many shops and offices on the streets leading into the CBD closing down. The main government offices have moved to a new complex at Leith Docks from the St James Centre in the CBD.

Problems of the CBD
1 Traffic congestion.
2 Parking restrictions.
3 Lack of space.
4 High costs.
5 Unsuitable buildings.

Solving the Problems
1 Restrictions on traffic, e.g. in the Old Town.
2 Building the Western Approach Road and Outer Ring Road.
3 Building multi-storey car parks.
4 Building office complexes and hotels in the CBD, e.g. around Festival Square.
5 Building centres for shopping, business, research, and light industry on the edge of the built-up area.

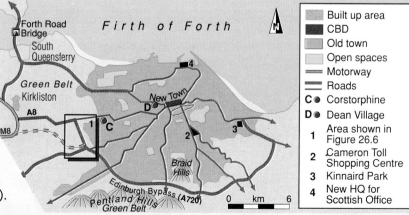

Figure 26.7 Developments in Edinburgh: location map

27 Living in Cities: Dundee

Growth of Dundee

With a population of 154 000, Dundee is Scotland's fourth largest city. From the twelfth century, it grew as a trading centre. It was helped by:

- fertile farming land nearby;
- a sheltered harbour on the Firth of Tay well placed to trade with Europe.

The city grew rapidly in the nineteenth century (see Figure 27.3). This was mainly the result of the jute industry. Jute is a tall swamp plant which grows in the Ganges delta. Dundee's mills made sacks and carpet backing from the imported jute. Thousands flocked to work in the mills, many coming from Ireland, from the Highlands, and from the surrounding countryside. Conditions in the mills (see Figure 27.1) were very hard for the mainly female workforce. The nearby tenement houses were poorly built, insanitary, and overcrowded.

Figure 27.1 It was a mainly female workforce in the Dundee jute mills

Figure 27.2 Late nineteenth century tenement housing being modernised

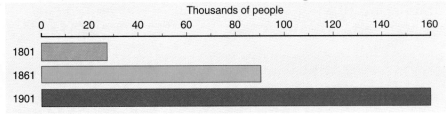

Figure 27.3 Population growth in nineteenth century Dundee

'Mary was eleven when she became a mill lassie. For the next fifteen years, hers was the world of the "knocker-up" who hammered on doors at five o'clock in the morning . . . Inside the long mill sheds, it was a world where the driving belts whirred from the steam-driven pulleys to the looms on which the weaving frames clattered. In the tiny, one-roomed home, with no supply of water or of lighting, and with no toilet, it was a world of no privacy whatever . . . The bath was a zinc tub on the floor once in a while. There were no public bath-houses any more than there were public lavatories, beyond the communal bucket closets placed for convenience next to the manure heap in the backyard.' (From *The Expendable Mary Slessor*, by James Buchan.)

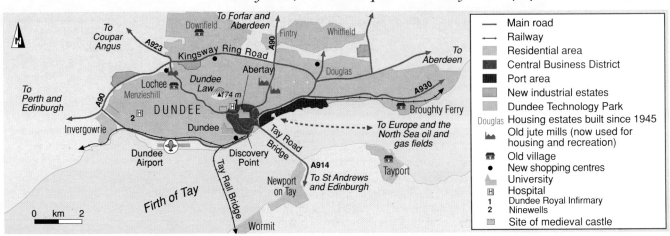

Figure 27.4 Aspects of Dundee

Changing Industry

Today Dundee no longer depends on 'the three Js' – jam, jute, and journalism. Textiles, including some jute, are still made, but in very modern factories, using far fewer people. Jam-making, which used local soft fruit, has gone. Journalism is still important: *The Dandy, Beano,* and *Sunday Post* are produced here.

Dundee's industry has been modernised and diversified.

- Tourists are being attracted by Discovery Point (Figure 27.6). New hotels have opened, and the city hosts many conferences.
- Dundee's harbour has been modernised, and is used as a base for the North Sea oil and gas industry.
- New high-technology science-based industries have been attracted to the city's industrial estates. Figure 27.5 shows Dundee Technology Park, on the western edge of the city. It has the advantages of:

Figure 27.5   Dundee Technology Park

- plenty of land for building;
- excellent communications;
- a skilled workforce;
- nearby universities and hospitals which carry out research.

Changing Housing

Many of the older tenements have been pulled down or renovated (see Figure 27.2). New housing estates, e.g. Whitfield, have been built on the outskirts, and these have also been modernised. Not everybody likes the tall tower blocks. Some of the older jute mills have been converted to houses (see Figure 27.7).

Figure 27.6   *The Discovery,* built in Dundee in 1910. It is now a major tourist attraction

Figure 27.7   A disused jute mill converted into modern housing

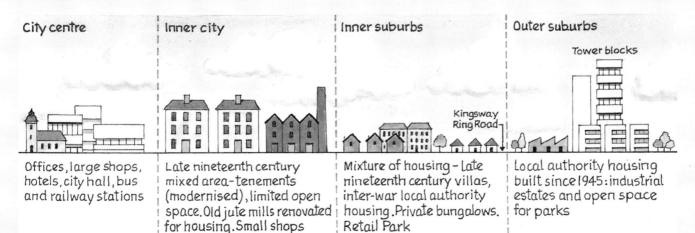

City centre	Inner city	Inner suburbs	Outer suburbs
Offices, large shops, hotels, city hall, bus and railway stations	Late nineteenth century mixed area-tenements (modernised), limited open space. Old jute mills renovated for housing. Small shops	Mixture of housing – Late nineteenth century villas, inter-war local authority housing. Private bungalows. Retail Park	Local authority housing built since 1945: industrial estates and open space for parks

Kingsway Ring Road

Tower blocks

Figure 27.8   Dundee townscape transect: from city centre to Fintry or Whitfield

28 Industry in Scotland

The making of goods, which is called secondary or manufacturing industry, was the main employer of people in Scotland for almost 200 years. Before the Industrial Revolution in the eighteenth century, most people worked in primary industry. That means that they worked on the land, in mines and quarries, and in fishing. Today in Scotland, most workers do not grow, produce, or make anything. Instead they provide a service in schools, hospitals, shops, banks, and offices as we saw in the case of Edinburgh.

Manufacturing industry is still important, but it is much changed. Scotland once relied on the heavy industries based on coal and steam power, and located on coalfields. They included the making of iron and steel, building locomotives and ships, and making chemicals. Today in Scotland, light industries have taken over. They use electricity for power, and can be located almost anywhere. The electronics industry, and making of leisurewear, medicines, and food products are examples of light industries.

Industry in Scotland has changed both in type and in location. The landscape of industry has also changed (Figure 28.1). Riverside locations in the country gave way first to polluted coalfield sites then to new locations on industrial parks.

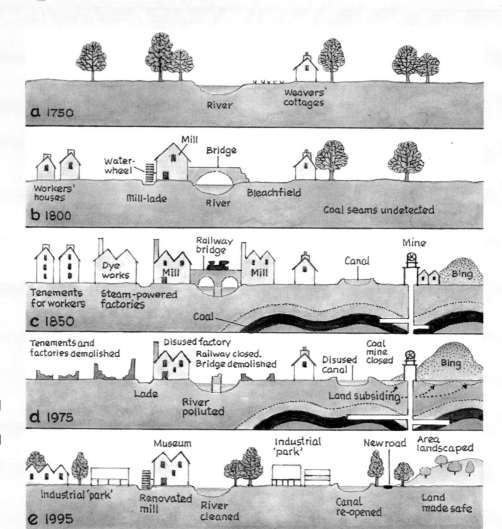

Figure 28.1 Changing industry in Central Scotland: locations and landscapes

Figure 28.2 An old industrial landscape: the derelict steel mills at Ravenscraig, Motherwell (now being demolished)

Figure 28.3 One of the many food depots and factories on Motherwell Food Park

Manufacturing Industry in Scotland Today

Manufacturing industry has changed both in location and in type. Nearness to airports and motorways is now significant. Grants and loans from the government are even more important. Great efforts are made to attract Japanese, American, and European firms to locate in Scotland. The new towns are good examples of sites of such new industrial developments, e.g. Livingston (Figure 28.4).

Traditional Industries

In small towns in the Scottish Highlands and in the Borders, there are still industries which flourish. Much of their output is exported to countries in Europe and others such as the USA and Japan. Some examples are:

- preserved and tinned foods, e.g. Baxter's of Fochabers;
- shortbread and cakes, e.g. Walker's of Aberlour;
- whisky distilling in many Highland towns;
- knitwear, e.g. Pringle of Hawick.

Pringle have generally flourished although they are far from the airports and motorways. They have smaller factories in other towns. They depend on other countries for their raw materials. Their products are of very high quality and value. They usually sell well to people who have the time and money to spend on leisurewear, e.g. for golf.

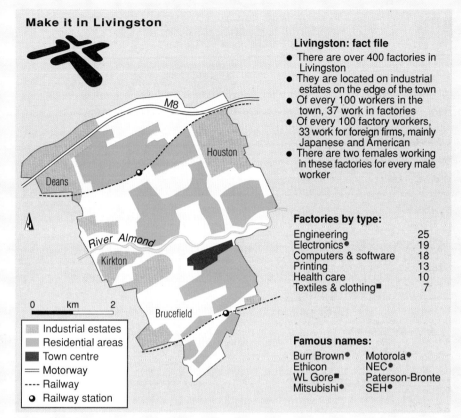

Figure 28.4 Livingston fact file

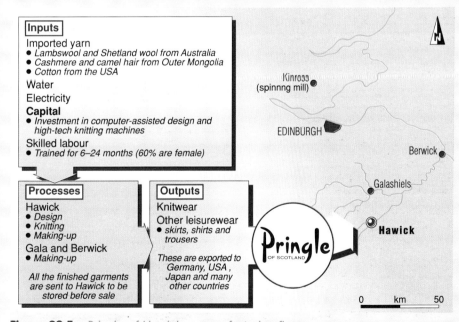

Figure 28.5 Pringle of Hawick: a manufacturing firm

All the materials needed are imported in the form of dyed yarn. Some of the lambswool from Australia is spun in Italy and imported to Hawick.

Labour shortages in Hawick resulted in some of the processes taking place in Berwick and Galashiels.

Pringle are part of a large group, Dawson International, with headquarters in Edinburgh. Pringle have offices in London, Stuttgart, New York, and Tokyo, to boost sales. Nick Faldo is among the famous golfers who help sell knitwear.

Industry in Scotland

Population

Balquhidder

The photograph of 11 children at Balquhidder Primary School (Figure 29.1) was taken about ten years ago. It illustrates several features of Scotland's population.

- Few people live in Scotland's countryside, i.e. it has a low **population density**
- Fewer children are being born, i.e. the **birth rate** in Scotland is low.
- Scotland's population is in decline. The school roll had fallen to only two in 1994, when it was decided to close the school.
- The population is becoming even more mixed.

At Balquhidder, in addition to the children born in Scotland, there were children from England, Germany, and Iceland. (At the same date, there were several much bigger primary schools in Glasgow where as many as 90 per cent of the children were of Asian, African, European, and American origin.)

The school is in the parish of Balquhidder. There were fewer than 600 people here, in an area of 209 km² (mostly high mountains), at the time of the 1991 census. The population density was therefore less than three people per km². This made it one of the emptiest parts of Scotland. The census also revealed that in Balquhidder:

Figure 29.1 Six nationalities at Balquhidder Primary School

Figure 29.2 Once small villages (*clachans*) occupied this empty glen above Loch Voil in Balquhidder parish

- the population had decreased by 41 since 1981;
- there were fewer males (249) than female (269);
- out of every 100 people, 20 were pensioners, and only 16 were at school;
- out of every 100 households, 29 consisted of one person;
- out of every 100 households, 80 had a car.

It can be seen from the facts below how typical Balquhidder is of Scotland as a whole.

Key Ideas about Scotland's Population

Scotland's population is:

- unevenly distributed (Figure 29.4), with densities per km² ranging from two in Sutherland to more than 3000 in Glasgow;
- Declining (Figure 29.3), with the population dropping to just over 5.1 million;
- Ageing. Out of every 100 people, only 20 were under the age of 16, and 18 were pensioners;
- Becoming more varied in origin.

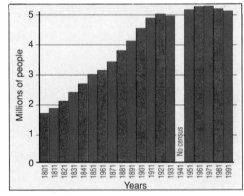

Figure 29.3 Scotland's population 1801–1991

Population Change

Scotland's population may have declined as a whole (Figure 29.3), however, parts of Scotland gained population (Figure 29.5), especially in attractive areas where people have chosen to retire. The districts around Aberdeen also benefited from the oil industry.

On the other hand, Shetland recently lost many people who had worked in oil-related construction. The more remote areas, the old industrial regions, and the four main cities all lost population. Despite these losses, most Scots still live in the central part of Scotland (Figure 29.4), mostly in urban areas, and especially the four main cities.

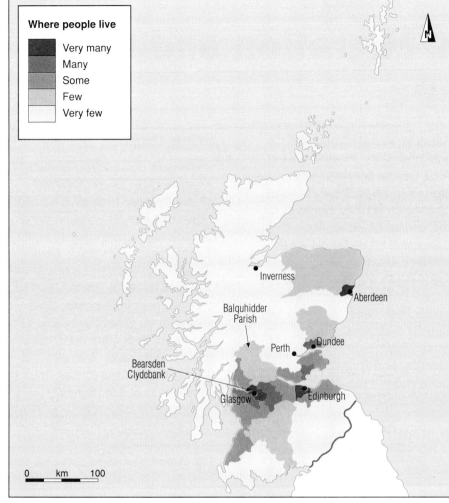

Figure 29.4 Where people live

The areas shown on Figure 29.4 with few or very few people had far less than 64 people per km² on average. There were as few as 2 per km² in Sutherland. These are areas of mountains and high hills. However, there are towns in the valleys and near the coats. Two of these towns, Perth and Inverness, are large, each with over 40 000 people.

In contrast to the mountains and the hills, many people were crowded together in the industrial areas in the lowlands of Central Scotland. Some urban areas have more than 1000 people per km², i.e. Edinburgh, Clydebank, Aberdeen, and Bearsden. Glasgow has lost many people, but there are still more than 3000 people for every km² of the city.

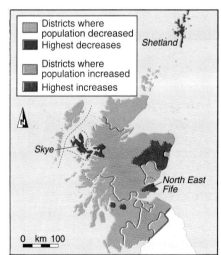

Figure 29.5 Population change 1981–1991

Migration in Scotland

People in Scotland have often migrated. In the eighteenth century, they began to leave the countryside to live in the towns. In the nineteenth century, many people left the Highlands to live in Central Scotland. Some had been evicted from their lands (see p 28). In the last part of the twentieth century, people have once again been on the move, as Figure 29.5 shows. In addition, many Scots still emigrate to other countries in search of a better life. To balance this, there are increasing numbers of people living in Scotland who were born elsewhere, e.g. in England and the Commonwealth countries.

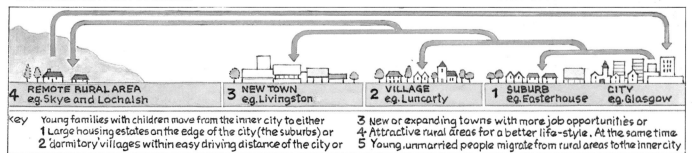

Figure 29.6 Migration in Scotland

Religion, Migration and the Landscape

About half of Scotland's population claim to have a religious belief. There are many beliefs. Often they have been brought by settlers, past and present.

Christian Beliefs

Figure 30.4 shows that most believers belong to a branch of the Christian church. Figure 30.3 shows that early Christianity spread from centres such as Iona, Whithorn, and Lindisfarne. Today the largest and most widespread branch is the Church of Scotland – the national church. Roman Catholics are the second largest group.

Figure 30.1 Modern Community Church. As population has grown, e.g. in New Towns, new churches like this one in Irvine New Town have been built

Figure 30.2 Remember the Sabbath. Sunday is a special day and the churches of Lewis and Harris object to plans to run Sunday ferries, or to carry out unnecessary work

Although found throughout Scotland, they are strongest in West Central Scotland since many Irish came there in the nineteenth century. Some of the smaller churches are concentrated in certain areas. The Free Church has its main following in the North West, Skye, Lewis, and Harris. With similar churches it tries to defend traditional Sunday observance. Methodists, Baptists, and Brethren are quite strong in Shetland, Orkney, and the fishing villages of the North East. The Episcopal Church is strongest in the east, especially the Borders.

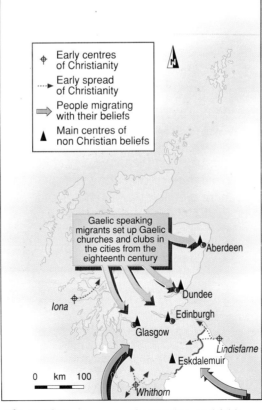

Early centres of Christianity

Early spread of Christianity

People migrating with their beliefs

Main centres of non Christian beliefs

Gaelic speaking migrants set up Gaelic churches and clubs in the cities from the eighteenth century

Aberdeen

Dundee

Iona

Edinburgh

Glasgow

Lindisfarne

Eskdalemuir

0 km 100

Whithorn

Figure 30.3 Aspects of migration and faith

Non-Christian Beliefs

Scotland nowadays is a multi-faith society. Many immigrants have brought their own non-Christian beliefs. Judaism grew in the nineteenth century when persecuted Jews came from Russia and eastern Europe. Since the 1950s, the synagogues in the main cities have been joined by Hindu temples, Sikh gurdwaras, and Muslim mosques. A small Buddhist community has grown up at Eskdalemuir.

	0	20	40	60	80	100%

Church of Scotland

Smaller Presbyterian churches, e.g. Free Church

Other Protestant churches, e.g. Baptist

Other Christian churches, e.g. Mormon

Roman Catholic

Non Christian, e.g. Hindu, Sikh, Muslim, Jewish

Figure 30.4 Religious beliefs in Scotland

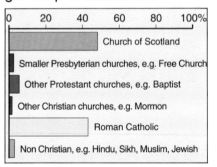

Figure 30.5 Tibetan Buddhist Centre, Kagyu Samye Ling, Eskdalemuir

Figure 30.6 Central Mosque, Gorbals, Glasgow

Figure 30.6   Monks and shaping the landscape 1100–1400

Saltworks were built by monks at Prestonpans. Sea water was evaporated leaving a coarse salt to preserve fish and meat	The earliest coal mines were started by the monks of Newbattle Abbey. Tunnels were dug into the coal along the valley of the River Esk. Monks from Dunfermline and Paisley Abbeys also started mining in the thirteenth century	Monks introduced sheep farming, especially in the Southern Uplands near Melrose. Wool was exported from Berwick	Hospices (a type of hospital) were built, often beside main roads eg. Soutra Hospice near Lauder

The Grange (the farm belonging to the Abbey)

Firth of Forth

River Esk

Coal

Abbey

In marshy areas the land was drained eg. in the Carse of Gowrie

Orchards were planted eg. at Dryburgh

Corn mills were built beside rivers to grind grain

Religion and the Landscape

Over thousands of years, the past and present beliefs of people can be seen in three ways.

- The shaping of the landscape.
- Places of worship.
- Place names on maps.

Shaping the Landscape

In the Middle Ages, monks from abbeys such as Melrose developed farming and industry in the countryside. See Figure 30.6.

Places of Worship

There are many reminders of worship before Christianity. At Callanish there is an impressive stone circle. About 5000 years ago, these large, heavy stones were erected by the farming families then living on Lewis. The weather was warmer then, and crops grew where there is damp peat today. The stone circle was a sort of temple, and people probably worshipped here. They may also have used the stones to follow the movements of the moon and sun.

Churches vary in size, style, building material, and how they are used. St Magnus Cathedral, Kirkwall, is a magnificent piece of architecture built from the twelfth century over a period

Figure 30.7   Melrose Abbey

of 300 years. Just as attractive are the smaller, simple churches found in the countryside. Ardgour Church (Argyll) is one of 40 designed by the famous engineer Thomas Telford. They were built in the nineteenth century in parts of the Highlands which needed new churches. Nowadays some church buildings are no longer used for worship. They may be used for anything from nightclubs, homes, cash and carry stores, to museums and concert halls.

Place Names on Maps

Many places in Scotland have religious names, for example:

Kil pheder, i.e. church of St Peter;
Kirk cudbright, i.e. church of St Cuthbert;
Paper Stour, i.e. great priest's island;
Drum chapel, i.e. chapel on the ridge;
Glen eagles, i.e. glen of the church (not eagles!);
Tober mory, i.e. well of the Virgin Mary.

Figure 30.8   Standing Stones, Callanish

Figure 30.9   St Magnus Cathedral at Kirkwall, Orkney

Figure 30.10   Ardgour 'Parliamentary' Church

Religion, Migration and the Landscape

Language, Dialect and Place Names

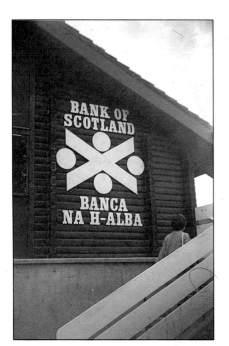

Figure 31.1 Bilingual signs are found on banks, shops and road sides in Gaelic-speaking areas

If these 100 people represent Scotland's population, only 2 can speak Gaelic

Ciamar a tha thu?

If these 100 people represent the population of the Western Isles, 68 can speak Gaelic

Gle'math
Tapadh leat

Figure 31.2 The Gaelic language in Scotland

Figure 31.3 Capercaille – a popular Gaelic folk band

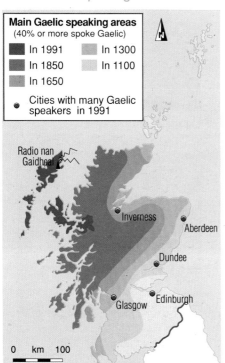

Main Gaelic speaking areas
(40% or more spoke Gaelic)

- In 1991
- In 1850
- In 1650
- In 1300
- In 1100
- Cities with many Gaelic speakers in 1991

Radio nan Gaidheal

Inverness
Aberdeen
Dundee
Glasgow
Edinburgh

0 km 100

Figure 31.4 Gaelic in retreat

Figure 31.5 A junior choir competing at the National Mod, a festival of Gaelic music and poetry

GAELIC

Signs (see Figure 31.1) tells us that Gaelic is spoken in parts of Scotland. Apart from the South East, Gaelic was once widespread, but Figure 31.4 shows how it has retreated. By 1991 the number of Gaelic speakers had fallen to 66000 people, mainly in the Western Isles, Skye and the North West Highlands.

WHY GAELIC DECLINED

- From the eighteenth century onwards, many Highlanders went to Central Scotland to work on farms and in factories. Many did not go back and their language died out. Even when they worked in the Lowlands for just a few months, they returned speaking at least some English.

- In many Highland homes, people were keen to learn English. Gaelic was seen as second best.

- Children were not encouraged to speak and study Gaelic in schools, especially after the 1872 Education Act.

ENCOURAGING GAELIC

Gaelic is more likely to be spoken by older people nowadays. The fear is that it may die out. So it is being encouraged in various ways.

- By setting up over 45 Gaelic-medium units in primary schools. As a result, in Skye for instance, the number of 5-15 year-olds who speak Gaelic is going up. Sometimes their parents have moved to Skye from England, or from non-Gaelic speaking parts of Scotland.

- By more Gaelic broadcasting, publishing and the influence of pop groups such as *Runrig* and *Capercaille*.

- By money and help from different organisations e.g. Comunn na Gàidhlig.

GÁIDHLIG

Tha comharraidhean (faic dealbh 31.1) a'g innseadh dhuinn gu bheil Gàidhlig air a bruidhinn am an cuid de dh-Alba. A fagail a mach an ear-dheas, bha Gàidhlig uair sgaoilte ach tha dealbh 31.4 a sealtainn mar a chaidh i air ais. Anns a 'bhleadhna naodh ceud deug agus ceithir fichead 'sa h-aon thuid aireamh na bha bruidhinn Gàidhlig gu tri fichead agus sia mile neach, anns a'mhór-chuid anns na h-Eileanan Siar, an t-Eilear Sgiathanach agus an iar-thuath na Gàidhealtachd.

CAR SON A'CHAIDH GÀIDHLIG AIR AIS

- Bho'n ochdamh linn deug 's air adhart chaidh mòran Ghaidheal do amheadhan Alba a dh-obair air tuatheanais agus taighean cearrde. Bha mòran nach do thill dhachaidh agus bhàsaich an cànan. Eadhon far an robh iad a'g obair anns a Ghalltachd air son beagan mhiosan, thi'll iad a bruidhinn beagan beurla, co-dhiù.

- Ann a' mòran dhachaidhean Gaidhealach bha daoine air son Beurla dh-ionnsachadh. Bha Gàidhlig air a faicinn mar rud gun fheum.

- Cha robh clann air am brosnachadh Gàidhlig a bhruidhinn no rannsachadh anns na sgoiltean, gu h-araidh an dèidh Achd an Fhoghlum, ochd ceud deag, tri fichead's dha dheug.

BROSNACADH GÀIDHLIG

An di ugh, mar is trice bith Gàidhlig air abruidhinn le seann daoine. 'Se eagal a th'ann guń bàsaich i, Mar sin tha i air a brosnachadh ann an iomadh doigh.

- A cur air chois da fhichead's coig aonead meadhan Gàidhlig ann am sgoiltean. Mar thoradh, anns an Eilean Sgiathanach mareisimpleir, tha an aireamh de chlann eadar coig agus coig-deug dh-aois a tha bruidhinn Gàidhlig a meudachadh. Uaireanan tha pàrantan air gluasad suig an Eilean Sgiathanach a' Sasainn, air neò a pairt de dh-Alba far nach eil iad a bruidhinn Gàidhlig.

- Le barrachd craobh -sgaoileadh Gàidhlig, foillseachadh agus buaidh nan còmhlain pop mar Run Rig agus Capercaille.

- Le airgead agus cuideachadh bho buidheannan eadar-dhealaichte-mar eisimpleir: Commun na Gàidhlig.

Language, Dialect and Place Names

Language, Dialect and Place Names

Scots: The Mither Tongue

As well as Gaelic, Norse, Scots, and English were among the languages once spoken in different parts of Scotland.

- Norse came with the Vikings and was mainly spoken in Shetland, Orkney, and Caithness. Like Gaelic, it gradually gave way to Scots and English.

- Scots is a rich language related to northern English. By the 1500s, it was the main language of Lowland Scotland, and it was Scotland's official language till 1707. It has gradually given way to English because:
  - the Bible was not translated into Scots;
  - speaking 'correct' English was believed to be important if you wanted to get on in the world;
  - schools did not encourage Scots (or Gaelic). It was banned from the classroom, but not the playground, as 'slang'.

Today we have several Scots dialects (see Figure 31.6). These are especially spoken in Shetland, Orkney, the North East, Ayrshire, and the Borders. There are now schemes, e.g. in schools in the North East to encourage the speaking and reading of 'Braid Buchan'. An extract is printed below. As with Gaelic, incomers are often interested in Scots dialects as well as traditional music and festivals.

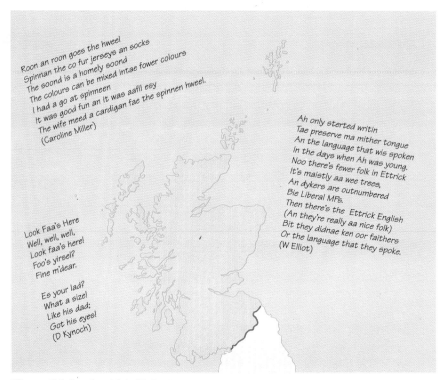

Roon an roon goes the hweel
Spinnan the co fur jerseys an socks
The soond is a homely soond
The colours can be mixed intae fower colours
I had a go at spinneen
It was good fun an it was aafil esy
The wife meed a cardigan fae the spinnen hweel.
(Caroline Miller)

Ah only started writin
Tae preserve ma mither tongue
An the language that wis spoken
In the days when Ah was young.
Noo there's fewer folk in Ettrick
It's maistly aa wee trees,
An dykers are outnumbered
Bie Liberal MPs.
Then there's the Ettrick English
(An they're really aa nice folk)
Bit they didnae ken oor faithers
Or the language that they spoke.
(W Elliot)

Look Faa's Here
Well, well, well,
Look faa's here!
Foo's yirsel?
Fine m'dear.

Es your lad?
What a size!
Like his dad;
Got his eyes!
(D Kynoch)

Figure 31.6 Scottish Dialects

'It was jist a skelp o the muckle furth,
A skylter o roch grun
Fin Granfadder's fadder bruke it in
Fae the hedder an the funn.
Granfadder sklatit barn an byre,
Brocht water to the closs,
Pat fail-dykes ben the bare brae face
An a cairt road tull the moss.'
(A verse of 'Bennygoak', by Flora Garry.)

New Scottish Languages

Immigrants still come to Scotland and bring their languages. People from Asia, for instance, have brought Urdu, Punjabi, Hindi, Gujerati, Cantonese, Hakka, and Vietnamese. Youngsters often go back to school on Saturday mornings, to keep up these languages and to learn about their traditions and religion.

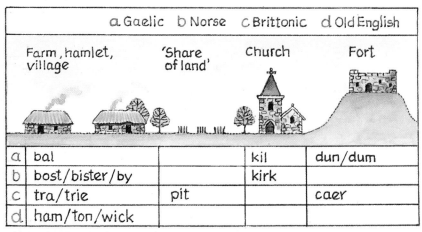

| | a Gaelic | b Norse | c Brittonic | d Old English |
	Farm, hamlet, village	'Share of land'	Church	Fort
a	bal		kil	dun/dum
b	bost/bister/by		kirk	
c	tra/trie	pit		caer
d	ham/ton/wick			

Figure 31.7 Settlement place names

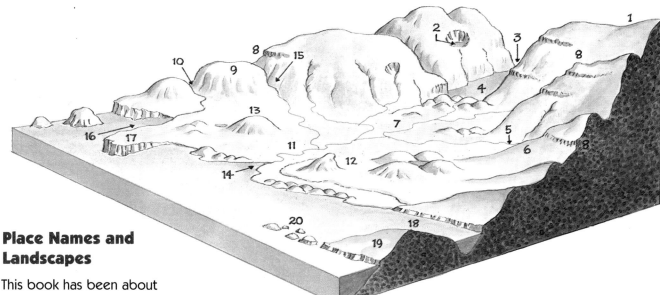

Place Names and Landscapes

This book has been about Scotland's changing landscapes. From the time of the first settlers, people have been altering the landscape of Scotland with their changing settlements and lifestyles. Place names are a good clue to the different peoples who have settled in Scotland over many years. On several pages, (e.g. pages 41, 65 and 67) in this book we have discussed place names. From them we can learn about the following.

- SETTLEMENT: place names help us work out why a settlement grew at a particular site (see Figures 18.5, 31.7 and page 41). For example,
  - farm – 'bal' (G) e.g. Ballinluig;
  - fort – 'dun' (G) e.g. Dunedin (Edinburgh).
- PEOPLE: we believe that 'Pit' tells us where the Picts lived e.g. Pitlochry and the suffix 'ton where Anglo Saxons lived e.g. Haddington.
- PHYSICAL FEATURES: Figure 31.8 and its key tells us some of the names of physical features in Scotland.

Number	Feature	Name	Example
1	Mountain	Beinn/Ben	Ben Nevis
2	Corrie	Coire	Coire Mhic Fhearchair
3	Deep narrow valley	Glen	Glen Lyon
4	Lake	Loch	Loch Lomond
5	Stream	Allt	Allt Leatham
6	Slope	Brae	Braes of Balquhidder
7	A broad valley	Strath	Strathmore
8	Crag	Craig	Craigellachie
9	A round hill	Meall	Meall Uaine
10	A pass	Bealach	Bealach nam Bo
11	A marshy plain	Carse	Carse of Gowrie
12	An isolated hill	Law	Largo Law
13	A hillock	Tulloch	Tullochcroisk
14	Mouth of a river	Aber/Inver	Abernethy/Inverness
15	A gorge	Cleuch	Green Cleuch
16	Bay	Voe/Vik	Sullom Voe, Wick
17	Headland	Ness	Tressness
18	Strait	Kyle	Kyle of Lochalsh
19	Island	Inch/Eilean	Inchcolm/Eilean nam Each
20	Small rocky islands	Skerries	Out Skerries

Figure 31.8 Place names and the physical landscape

Glossary

Acid rain rain which contains chemicals from the smoke caused by burning fossil fuels at power stations and factories.

Ageing population a population in which the number of people over 60 is increasing, while the number of people under 16 is decreasing.

Agricultural Revolution the name given to the changes in farming from the seventeenth century which gradually resulted in improved crops, crop rotation, new breeds of animals, and an increased use of machinery.

Arable farming the cultivation of crops.

Birth rate the number of births in a year per 1000 of total population.

Bypass a road which is built round a busy town or city to prevent traffic jams in the centre.

Capital money which is needed to start a business, e.g. a farm, factory, or hotel.

Chambered cairn a pre-historic stone-built tomb, often built into a hillside.

Climate what the weather is like from season to season and year to year.

Container terminal the part of a seaport where containers (large rectangular metal boxes of the same size) are stored on a quay, and transferred to and from ships, lorries, and trains.

Continent a very large and clearly defined area of land, e.g. Africa. Most of the seven continents are divided into different countries.

Crag and tail A hard mass of rock – the crag – which protected the softer rock beyond it – the tail – from being eroded by an ice sheet.

Detour a journey which does not take the shortest or straightest route.

Drought a long continuous period of dry weather.

Drumlin (Figure 4.5) a low, smooth, rounded hill found in lowland areas. It was formed by ice sheets, and consists of clay with stones.

Estuary (Figure 8.2) the broad mouth of a river where it meets the sea.

Evaporation the process by which water is changed into water vapour by the heat of the sun.

Fault line a deep crack in the earth's crust, along which the surface has moved, vertically or horizontally. This can cause earthquakes and tremors.

Flood plain (Figure 24.3) the level area beside a river which is often flooded when the river overflows.

Ford a shallow part of a river where people could cross without a bridge.

Fossil fuel fuels, e.g. coal, gas, and oil, formed over millions of years from the remains of plants and animals.

Global warming the warming of the earth's atmosphere by carbon dioxide produced from the burning of fossil fuels.

Green belt an area of undeveloped land encircling a town.

Heavy industries manufacturing industry which needs large quantities of often bulky raw materials.

Hydro-electric power energy generated by the force of falling water.

Ice Age the last time that ice sheets covered much of Europe and North America.

Industrial estates a district of purpose-built factories with supporting services, often at the edge of a town or city.

Glossary

Industrial Revolution the name given to the changes in industry from the eighteenth century onwards. This involved an increasing use of machinery, steam power, and the building of factories.

Land use conflict disagreement by different people over how to use the land.

Light industry manufacturing industry which produces goods light in weight and high in value.

Motte and bailey castle (Figure 8.3) a twelfth century castle, the main tower of which was built on a large mound (or motte) of earth. The lower, walled courtyard (or bailey) contained houses for servants and soldiers, stables, bakehouse, etc.

New town a new planned town, designed to provide housing and jobs for people from overcrowded cities.

Non-renewable resources which cannot be used again once consumed.

Peninsula (Figure 1.4) an area of land with water on three sides.

Petro-chemicals a branch of the chemical industry which uses oil as its raw material.

Plain (Figure 8.2) a wide area of low, level land.

Plateau the almost level top of an upland area.

Population density the average number of people in an area for every square kilometre of land.

Primary industry economic activity concerned with the extraction of raw materials including farming, fishing, forestry, mining and quarrying.

Quay waterfront, made of wood, stone, or concrete, in a port. Ships tie up at quays to be loaded and unloaded.

Rain shadow an area of relatively low rainfall to the side of uplands sheltered from the wind.

Reclamation improving land by draining marshland or getting rid of industrial waste.

Renewable resources which can be used again if carefully looked after.

Residential a residential area is an area where people reside or live.

Ridge (Figure 25.1) a long, narrow, steep-sided upland.

Ro-ro terminal the part of a port where cars and lorries roll on and roll off ferries.

Secondary or manufacturing industry the creation of finished products from raw materials.

Seismograph an instrument which measures and records the strength of shock waves in the earth's crust caused by earthquakes, sometimes far away.

Service sector involves work in offices, shops, hotels, schools, hospitals and transport to provide services for people.

Set-aside an EU scheme to reduce the food mountains which pays farmers not to grow particular crops.

Site the position of something in physical, local terms.

Spit a ridge of sand running away from the coast.

Tenement a multi-storey stone building common in Scottish cities. It may be from 80 to 140 years old, with many flats linked by a common stairs.

Tombolo a spit which joins an offshore island to the mainland.

Tundra a type of vegetation including a rich variety of mosses, lichens, small bushes, flowering plants and dwarf trees, usually found on lowlands near the Arctic Ocean, but also on the highest mountains in Scotland.

Urban an urban area is a large built-up area, i.e. a town or city.

Volcano an opening of the earth's crust out of which magma, ash and gases erupt.

Weather day to day changes in rainfall and temperature.

Scotland: new local Government areas, 1996

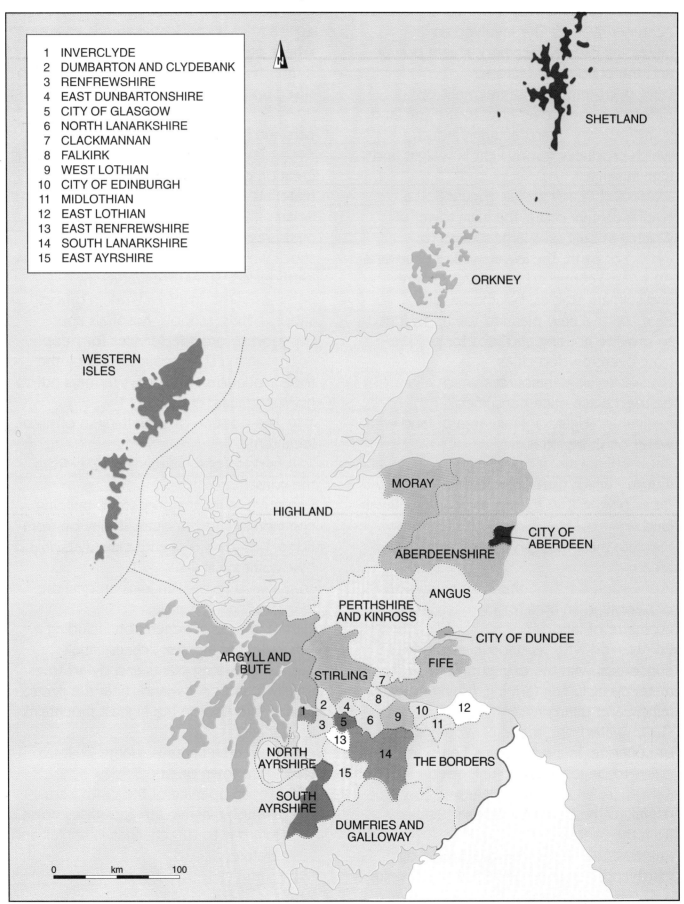

1 INVERCLYDE
2 DUMBARTON AND CLYDEBANK
3 RENFREWSHIRE
4 EAST DUNBARTONSHIRE
5 CITY OF GLASGOW
6 NORTH LANARKSHIRE
7 CLACKMANNAN
8 FALKIRK
9 WEST LOTHIAN
10 CITY OF EDINBURGH
11 MIDLOTHIAN
12 EAST LOTHIAN
13 EAST RENFREWSHIRE
14 SOUTH LANARKSHIRE
15 EAST AYRSHIRE

SHETLAND

ORKNEY

WESTERN
ISLES

HIGHLAND

MORAY

ABERDEENSHIRE

CITY OF
ABERDEEN

ANGUS

PERTHSHIRE
AND KINROSS

CITY OF DUNDEE

FIFE

ARGYLL AND
BUTE

STIRLING

NORTH
AYRSHIRE

SOUTH
AYRSHIRE

THE BORDERS

DUMFRIES AND
GALLOWAY

0   km   100